INSIGHT COMPACT GUIDE

Ma

GREAT LITTLE GUIDES

Compact Guide: Madrid is the ultimate quick-reference guide to the Spanish capital. It tells you all you need to know about Madrid's attractions, from the Palacio Real to the Museo del Prado and Plaza Mayor to Parque del Retiro, taking in the bars and taverns of the old city and the sparkling facades of the new.

This is one of 120 Compact Guides, which combine the interests and enthusiasms of two of the world's best known information providers: Insight Guides, whose titles have set the standard for visual travel guides since 1970, and Discovery Channel, the world's premier source of nonfiction television programming.

Star Attractions

An instant reference to some of Madrid's most popular tourist attractions to help you set your priorities.

Plaza Mayor p21

Palacio Real p29

Cable car across the river p32

Casa de Lope de Vega p41

El Rastro flea market p45

Parque del Retiro p50

Museo del Prado p57

Jardín Botánico p60

Centro de Arte Reina Sofía p60

Toledo p66

Puerta de Europa p64

MADRID

Introduction

Places

Culture

Leisure

Practical Information

Madrid – At the Heart of the Bull

Opposite:
Don Quixote salutes

The map of Spain is often compared with a bull's hide laid out in the sun to dry. On this basis Madrid would be the heart of the bull, not only because all the roads in Spain meet up outside the town hall on the Puerta del Sol, but also because all the country's political, social and cultural impulses start from here.

It has not always been like that. Up until the 1970s, the city that is now noisy, vibrant and throbbing with life, was as peaceful as a graveyard. Hordes of night revellers now gather where once the night watchman kept a lonely vigil. Until relatively recently the people were cowed by the authoritarian control of the Franco regime. Today the whole gamut of opinions and lifestyles co-exist. To most Spaniards, having a good time is not something for fiestas and weekends, it is a right. Madrid is a place where, so long as decorum is observed, people tend to do as they please. Ride your noisy motorbike on the pavement? Leave the dog out all night? Drive around in the early hours with the car stereo at full volume? No-one will complain. *Madrileños* are tolerant people; in fact a touch of anarchy often prevails. Life here is lived to the hilt. Nightlife in Paris or Rome would be dull by comparison.

Don't expect people to speak English: they won't. Spain's long years of isolation have left a lingering suspicion of foreigners. Behind those sometimes daunting stares lie generous hearts and a civilised approach to life. After all, *madrileños* have always welcomed outsiders. Without immigrants from all parts of Spain and beyond, nothing would have emerged that in any way resembles the legendary *castizo* traditions. Meaning pure-blooded and authentic, the word encapsulates the *madrileño* character. There is no question about it, modern Madrid is proud of its great diversity. It is precisely for that reason that the bull's heart is beating stronger than ever.

Alfresco dining

Residents of Puerta del Sol

Situation and landscape

Madrid (pop. 3.1m), the capital of Spain and of the autonomous region of Madrid (*Comunidad de Madrid*; pop. 5.03m), lies at the heart of the vast Castilian plateau *(meseta)* and right in the centre of Spain. The historic core of the Iberian peninsula extends over the autonomous regions of Castilla-Léon (Old Castile), Castilla-La Mancha (New Castile) and Extremadura. Covering an area of over 200,000 sq km (75,000 sq miles), this region occupies about 40 percent of Spanish territory. The Castilian mountain range divides the *meseta* into a northern and southern half. Rising from the Sierra de Guadarrama mountain range about 90km (56

miles) north of the city are peaks which reach a height of 2,400m (7,500ft). During the summer day-trippers often head for the cooler air on these slopes, while in the winter it is even possible to ski here. The relief of the *meseta* also has an effect on the city's outward face. Situated at an average height of 650m (2,130ft), Madrid is the highest European capital. The gentle ups and downs of many streets in the Old Town reflect the contours of the high plateau, but there are no natural commanding spots within the city's boundaries. Although the steep slopes above the Manzanares river form a sort of terrace, *madrileños* love to poke fun at its meagre flow. They say it suffers from *mal de piedra* or 'stone disease'.

The people of Madrid are proud of the city's many open spaces, which occupy almost half of the total surface area of 600 sq km/230 sq miles (Madrid autonomous region 8,000 sq km/3,100 sq miles). The many tree-lined boulevards and roads, especially in the newer quarters, help to create a sense of space, but the large parks such as the Retiro, the Parque del Oeste and the huge Casa de Campo in the Manzanares valley cannot prevent the pollution from the huge volumes of traffic from rising to alarming levels.

Relaxing in Parque del Retiro

The sacrosanct siesta

Climate and when to go

While it is true that Madrid lies on the same line of latitude as Naples or Istanbul, the *meseta* can offer nothing resembling the mild Mediterranean-style climate. *Del invierno al inferno* or 'from winter straight into hell' is how the locals often describe the continental inland climate of extremes typical of central Castile.

If you have endured a numbing rainy and windy winter's day, then you will, almost certainly, be wanting a hotel with a fully functioning heating system. Frost and snow are rare. The icy wind from the Sierra may occasionally blow in a few white flakes, but they never stay around for long. In the nearby Avila province, on the other hand, whole villages can sometimes be cut off from the outside world for days by blizzards.

Flowers that bloom in the spring

Spring and autumn bring pleasant, moderately warm sunny days, but provide only a short interlude. During the summer, temperatures regularly rise to over 40°C (104°F). The heat can sometimes be unbearable, particularly in late afternoon when the asphalt and concrete have heated up. If you do not have to work, then you leave Madrid for this part of the year. *Madrileños* prefer to spend their summer holidays (*veranear* in Spanish) on the Costa Blanca or on the cooler north coast. Many restaurants, shops and smaller museums close for the holiday period.

As a consolation for the heat-resistant tourists and those residents who have no choice but to stay put, the summer promises a rich and varied cultural programme,

Royal Horseguards

including the music, theatre, ballet, film and various open-air events of the *Verano de la Villa* (summer arts festival). With so many local people fleeing the capital in the summer, there is noticeably less traffic congestion, the cafés along Paseo de la Castellana are livelier at night and the numbers visiting the Prado Museum and the Thyssen-Bornemisza collection lower than usual. The cool museums make perfect refuges from the intense daytime heat.

Population

Lo que menos hay en Madrid son madrileños or 'at least Madrid has the *madrileños*'.

Since Felipe II moved his court in the 16th century from Valladolid to the heart of his empire, Madrid has continued to be a city of immigrants. Whether they come from Andalusia, Asturias, the Basque region, Extremadura or Galicia, those who have moved to the capital in search of work since the beginning of the 20th century originate mainly from the poorer regions of Spain.

Madrid underwent massive growth when Franco's industrialisation plans led to serious unemployment in the provinces. Between 1950 and 1970 the population in the *Comunidad* increased from 1.9 to 4.8 million. A reversal of this trend was first noted in the 1990s. By 1998 about 130,000 young *madrileños* had turned their backs on the traffic congestion and high rents and settled in the housing estates *(urbaniziciones)* on the northern outskirts.

Let the entertainment begin: at a bullfight

Many immigrants from Latin America, the Caribbean and Africa have also made their homes in Madrid. At least 130,000 foreigners live in the city, about 30,000 of them illegally. Like the Spanish migrants, the new arrivals have brought their own gastronomy, festivals and customs, thereby enriching even further the city's cultural diversity. Anyone who listens in on the contemporary music scene is sure to hear the Latin influence. Cuban salsa, Colombian cumbia, merengue from the Dominican Republic and tango from Argentina have been the repertoire in the city's clubs for a long time. Gypsies *(gitanos)* form a significant minority but most are now permanently settled.

Like everywhere else in Spain, Madrid society has changed dramatically since the *transición* to democracy. The birth rate is similar to that in most northern European countries and the influence of the once all-powerful church is waning. While it is true that 96 percent of the population regard themselves as Catholics, only a third of them are regular churchgoers.

The traditional role of women has undergone a remarkable change since 1975. During the Franco period, married women were not even allowed to open a bank account without their husband's permission, let alone earn money. Now women make up one third of the workforce.

The true nature of the *madrileño* soul is the source of much speculation, not least by the *madrileños* themselves. Ramón Gómez de la Serna, a dedicated observer of his fellow *madrileños*, wrote that they are a 'collection of imaginative people who know how to live the miracle of life and know that laughter is something very serious'. One thing is certain: the concept of *el madrileño castizo*, the true *madrileño,* does exist. But the faces are too varied. Is it the civil servant with the brightly-polished black shoes? The elegant young manager with his mobile phone? The blind lottery ticket seller on the Puerta del Sol? The extravagantly-dressed society queen in designer wear? Or perhaps it is the scruffy student from Lavapiés or the cleaner from the Caribbean? What unites them all is a kind of love-hate relationship with the chaos which envelops their daily life. Clearly this informs the vitality, the flexibility and the ready wit of the *madrileños*. But at the same time they are proud of the everyday madness that drives

On song and on parade

the city on. They grin and then declare: *aqui vivimos de película* or 'we live our life as if it's a film.' In Madrid you too can join in the non-stop cinema.

Madrileño originals

Him: an upright gait, moustache, slicked-back hair, dazzling white shirt, short jacket with silver buttons, tight trousers, pointed shoes, piercing eyes. Her: laced blouse, covered by a black silk *mantilla*, colourful mid-calf dress over several layers of petticoats, hair stylishly pinned up, husky voice and with an inviting look on her face.

The pair, called *Manolo y Manola*, were born in Lavapiés and they turn up at every fiesta in the quarter.

The name for these caricatures from the poor side of town originated during the 17th century when converted Jews christened their first-born Emanuel, usually shortened to Manolo. Out of the *barrio*'s long-established residents, *gitanos* and new immigrants from Andalusia, Murcia or La Mancha, emerged a new breed: the men were proud of their lowly origins, impetuous and amorous, the girls saucy and quick-witted, the quintessential *manolo* and *manola*.

Madrileño originals adorn the Laboratorio Juanje

During the 18th century, the manner and dress of these smart underdogs, now referred to as *majo* and *maja* (meaning attractive, pretty), became the fashion model on the smarter side of town. Aristocratic *duquesas* and *condes* suddenly developed a taste for the styles adopted by the market girls and coachmen. Goya even went as far as to portray the woman who many believe was his mistress, the Duchess of Alba, as *maja*, once fully clothed, once naked. The second led to his appearance before the Inquisition.

During the 19th century, the image of the *majos* changed. They were now known as *chulos* or *chulapos,* shady characters often modelled on the bandit Luis Candelas, Madrid's answer to Robin Hood. The archetypal *chulo* now wears a check waistcoat, neckerchief, has a malicious tongue, speaks in a strong Madrid dialect and is quick to reach for the stiletto.

The economy

If you are to believe the statistics, then since the demise of the Franco era Madrid has in economic terms been on a permanent upward path. Madrid's rising contribution to the Gross Domestic Product (GDP) is currently 16.6 percent, a share beaten only by Catalonia. Constant rival Barcelona, however, has recently found that it is losing out. IFEMA, the Madrid trade fair, located in the new Juan Carlos I exhibition complex (near Barajas airport), now welcomes some 3 million visitors each year and has become the country's most important commercial event.

Along the Calle Mayor

As you would expect in a modern capital city, the

service sector is responsible for the major share of economic output (72 percent). Industry contributes 19 percent of the city's GDP. The building industry comes in third with 8.5 percent, while agriculture (0.2 percent) is understandably of little importance. Business does, however, play a big part. A quarter of all Spanish shopping centres are situated within the *Comunidad de Madrid* region.

Tourism attracts nearly 5m guests, 66 percent being business travellers. The city boasts 50,000 hotel beds, about a half of which are in the 4- and 5-star category. There are about 1,900 *hostales* and *pensiones*.

Taking in the sights on Plaza de Toros

Despite all the success stories emanating from official sources, life in Madrid has not improved for everybody. The Spanish economy is still weighed down by high levels of unemployment. Keeping inflation low and reducing the national debt continue to be key economic targets. The wages of ordinary working people have not kept pace with price increases. The future is especially bleak for young people without skills or qualifications. Prostitution, drug addiction and crime have afflicted many of those with poor job prospects.

Smart apartments

A clear north-south divide characterises the social make-up of the city. Anyone who has made it chooses to live in the fashionable Salamanca quarter *(see page 49)*. The middle-class families now prefer the northern outskirts, where it is possible to buy a terraced house *(chalé)*. The lower-middle classes gravitate towards the cheaper, and in places rather run-down apartments in Malasaña or Lavapiés *(see page 37* and *43)*. Students and new arrivals from Morocco or Latin America also find reasonably-priced accommodation there.

In a belt around the south of the city lie many characterless dormitory towns such as Carabanchel, Vallecas and Villaverde, which were built during the 1950s for newcomers from the rural regions. These are now where the majority of the low-paid workers live. Not unlike the *favelas* of Rio de Janeiro are the shanty towns and permanent campsites beside the main arterial roads and under motorway bridges in the southern and eastern suburbs. The *chabolas* (tin huts) are home to thousands of illegal immigrants, gypsies and drug addicts.

The coat-of-arms

Villa y Corte

He could have chosen from such magnificent towns as Toledo, Salamanca, Segovia and Valladolid, so why on earth did Felipe II pick such an insignificant spot in the heart of the *meseta* as the seat for his court? What was it that was so attractive to a man who at that time was one of the most powerful rulers in the world? Why go for a small town named Majrit with a population of about 3,000? Perhaps he was looking for political neutrality, perhaps he wanted to turn over a new leaf in the history books or maybe he was rather taken by its position as the geographical centre of the country. But since 1561 Madrid has wanted to be known officially as *Villa y Corte* or 'market town and court'. The *madrileños* continue to use this expression which describes their town with a hint of gentle irony. It has grown up quickly, it has improvised, but somehow it has remained a town.

The head of state, now King Juan Carlos I, has traditionally ruled from the Palacio de la Zarzuela (Bosques del Pardo). Of course, the two parliaments *(cortes generales)*, the Senate and the Chamber of Deputies *(see page 39)*, meet in the capital too. The prime minister runs the country from his office in the Moncloa quarter, where all the other ministries and high court buildings are based.

What was once a highly centralised state, has now devolved powers to the provinces. Madrid is indeed Spain's capital, but it is only one out of 17 autonomous regions (*comunidades autónomas*), each with its own government and wide-ranging responsibilities, including education, culture and tourism. The *Comunidad de Madrid* breaks down into 179 municipalities *(municipios)*, of which the smallest, Madarcos in the Sierra de Guadarrama, has only 33 inhabitants, and the largest (Madrid) has 3.1 million inhabitants. The municipality of Madrid itself consists of 21 districts.

The predominant political force during the past 14 years throughout Spain has been the PSOE *(Partido Socialista Obrero Español)* under the leadership of prime minister Felipe González. But in 1996, following a series of corruption and bugging scandals, the PP *(Partido Popular)* under José María Aznar, won power at the head of a coalition. His party's success was set to continue when it won the March 2000 election with a clear overall majority.

Ministry of Agriculture

Flying the flags

Civil War memorial

Eternal flame

The forgotten war

1996 marked the 60th anniversary of the Spanish Civil War, an event which split the whole nation into two warring halves. But nowadays this dark chapter in Spanish history is hardly mentioned. It was as though upon the death of General Franco the nation signed a pact of silence to prevent the national trauma from deepening ever further.

The battle for the capital began on 18 July 1936 when *El Caudillo*, as he was called, launched his uprising against the Republican administration. The Popular Front government immediately distributed arms to Madrid workers. On 20 July the barracks in what is now Parque del Oeste were stormed and the hated Nationalists lynched. The short summer of anarchy, however, was not to last long. Franco's troops advanced from the south and carried out massacres that put the 'red terror' in the shade. By October the Nationalist troops were ready to take Madrid. The government fled to Valencia, while Mussolini and Hitler supplied soldiers and aircraft so that the bombing could begin.

When in November the onslaught started, the militias, together with the anarchists under Buenaventura Durruti and the International Brigades, used Soviet arms to repulse the attackers in bloody house-to-house combat. But the *Franquistas* dug in at the Casa de Campo park and bombarded the town with heavy artillery. Despite hunger and deprivation, the Madrid Republicans fought on. Communist leader, Dolores Ibárruri (*La Pasionaria*) issued the instruction: *¡No pasarán!* – They will not pass! The front, which the soldiers reached by tram, hardly moved for the rest of the war. The battle for Madrid was decided elsewhere. A way out of the impasse was finally achieved when Colonel Casado surrendered unconditionally to General Franco. On 1 April 1939 the *Generalísimo* marched into the capital, but the killing went on. By 1944 at least

200,000 Republicans had died as part of the political cleansing process and at least 400,000 went into exile.

Noise capital of Europe

It is a normal morning on Gran Vía. The din from six lanes of traffic resonates between the concrete façades of the multi-storey office blocks. Noisy diesel buses, screeching brakes at red traffic lights, ear-piercing moped exhausts, the cries of the lottery ticket sellers, the penetrating squeal of an ambulance siren, the shrill whistle of a traffic policeman – these are the routine sounds of the typical Madrid street. A recent European Union study revealed that no other European city is anywhere near as loud. A level of 70 decibels – above which the ear can suffer permanent damage – is exceeded in half of all the roads in urban Madrid for more than 10 hours a day. The blame lies primarily with the 1.2 million cars, whose average speed in the city centre is a meagre 14kmph (9mph).

But the never-ending background noise does not seem to worry the city's hardened residents. They either don't hear it or else they compensate by making even more noise. The TV in the bar is turned up, the hand reaches impatiently for the car horn – and everyone shouts. Like all creatures on earth, the *madrileños* have simply adjusted to their environment.

Concentration amid the cacophony

Bullfighting

Spain's *Fiesta Nacional* seems to be flourishing as never before. In one recent year there were 2,500 *corridas*, a record in the history of bullfighting. It is true that many Spaniards regard this form of popular entertainment as an anachronism and animal rights campaigners in Spain and abroad condemn the sport as butchery. But the reality is that both teenagers and women are flocking to the arenas to cheer on their heroes in the red *capas*. The greatest idol among the *matadores*, Jesulín de Ubrique, who retired in 1999, occasionally gave free galas for his female fans, who then showered him with their underwear.

Heroes of the corrida

Hardened observers, such as the respected *El País* commentator, Joaquín Vidal, regard the boom in bullfighting with growing scepticism. The *figuras*, the great bullfighters, are only after the big money and are going into the ring too often and reducing the ancient drama to an undignified mass spectacle. Some of the private TV channels broadcast the bloody bullfights as pure entertainment, ignoring the high arts of *tauromaquia*. To create greater excitement, overweight and tame bulls *(ratitas* or little mice*)* are thrust into the ring, their horns blunted so that the *torero* is not put at risk. The highest award the *matador* can receive, the bull's ear, has been debased. In 1997 star bullfighter, Enrique Ponce, won 159 *orejas*.

Historical Highlights

Early developments

Stone and pottery finds on the banks of the Río Manzanares prove that as early as 25,000BC semi-nomadic farmers had settled in the area around Madrid. From 900BC Iberians related to North African Berbers mix in central Spain with Celts from the northeast. The resulting ethnic group is known as the Celtiberians. There is no evidence of any larger settlement on the site of present Madrid during the period of Roman domination (50BC to 4th century AD) or during the Visigoth era (from about AD400 to 711). The Visigoths choose Toledo as their capital.

711 Start of the Arab-Berber invasion of the Iberian peninsula which extends as far as the Río Duero north of Madrid; Córdoba is capital of the Moorish empire.

852–886 To protect Toledo, Mohammed I builds a castle *(alcázar)* on the site of the present royal palace. The walled town *(medina)* is called Majrit (Madrid), meaning 'settlement with abundant water'.

9th–10th centuries Southern and central Spain enjoy a period of cultural and economic prosperity under the tolerant Moors. Christian resistance develops in the northern kingdoms.

1085 When the Moorish empire breaks up into separate principalities, Madrid is captured by Alfonso VI of Castile-León.

1109 A siege of Madrid by Berber prince, Jusuf, fails when plague breaks out among his soldiers.

1202 Alfonso VIII grants Madrid special rights *(fueros)* and elevates the village to a market town, giving it a degree of autonomy.

1309 The Castilian parliament *(Cortes de Castilla)* of Fernando IV sits in Madrid.

1346 Alfonso XI allows the formation of a city council. Several Castilian kings reside temporarily in Madrid.

1469 The marriage between Isabella of Castile and Ferdinand of Aragón (the 'Catholic Monarchs') unites both kingdoms.

1478 Start of the Spanish Inquisition.

1492 Granada, the last Moorish bastion, falls. Start of the systematic persecution and expulsion of Jews.

1499 4,000 Moors are baptised at Toledo by order of Ferdinand and Isabella.

1516–55 Carlos I of Spain, Emperor Charles V, rules Spain from an itinerant court, initiating the Habsburg dynasty. The Spanish colonial empire expands under his rule.

1561 Carlos's son, Felipe II, moves his court from Toledo to Madrid, which then becomes the capital. Madrid has 3,000 inhabitants, with most living in houses made from clay.

1563–84 Building of El Escorial palace.

1571 Battle of Lepanto against the Turks gives Spain control over the Mediterrranean.

1588 Defeat of the Spanish Armada by the English fleet destroys Spain as a sea power.

1609 Felipe III banishes the *moriscos* (converted Muslims) and allows burning of heretics on the Plaza Mayor.

1700 Carlos II, the last Spanish Habsburg, dies childless. The Spanish War of Succession between the Austrian Habsburgs and the French Bourbons ends in 1713 with the Treaty of Utrecht. Philip of Anjou, as Felipe V, becomes the first Bourbon ruler.

1734 Madrid's *alcázar* is destroyed by fire.

1737–64 Building of new royal palace on the site of the *alcázar*.

1759–88 The Bourbon king, Carlos III, 'Madrid's best mayor', rules as an enlightened despot, strengthening the crown's authority over the church by restricting the power of the Inquisition and expelling the Jesuits. The city landscape is changed as a result of his love of neo-classical architecture. A sewage system and street lighting are introduced and streets are paved.

1808 Charles IV abdicates and French army under Napoleon enters Madrid; on 2 May Madrid rises against the French but the revolt is brutally quashed, and on 3 May leading protagonists are executed.

1808–14 War of Independence (Peninsula War) during which Napoleon's brother Joseph Bonaparte, rules. The French are defeated.

1814–33 Fernando VII restores absolute rule.

1819 Opening of the Prado museum, based on the royal collection.

1833–76 Power struggles between the liberals and ultra-conservatives (three 'Carlist Wars'). Cholera epidemic in Madrid.

1851 The first railway line in Spain, between Madrid and Aranjuez, is opened.

1873 Dictator Amelio Castelar proclaims the First Spanish Republic.

1874–85 During the reign of King Alfonso XII, Madrid's first telephone lines installed and tram service opened.

1898 The loss of the last overseas colonies leads to economic depression and social unrest.

1921 Madrid's metro system opens.

1923 Military dictatorship under General Miguel Primo de Rivera tolerated by the king.

1931 Republicans win popular election. The Second Republic is proclaimed and Alfonso XIII goes into exile.

1936 The left-wing Popular Front wins parliamentary elections, but Spanish society is dangerously polarised. Uprising led by Nationalist General Franco.

1936–9 600,000 die in the Spanish Civil War, which ends in Nationalist victory. Battle rages around Madrid for three years.

1939–75 Dictatorship under General Franco. The church, the military and the landowners hold the reins of power throughout the country.

1955 Spain joins the United Nations.

1965–73 Strikes and student protests in Madrid.

1975 After the death of *El Caudillo*, parliamentary democracy is restored in Spain. King Juan Carlos I becomes the head of state, re-establishing the Bourbon monarchy. Spain is reintegrated into Europe.

1976 The first issue of *El País* newspaper goes on sale on 4 May.

1977 Adolfo Suárez, a moderate conservative, becomes prime minister after the first free elections.

1979–86 Madrid enjoys a cultural flowering under socialist mayor, Enrique Tierno Galván.

1981 Attempted military coup by a Guardia Civil officer fails after congress held at gunpoint. Picasso's *Guernica* is brought to Spain in accordance with the artist's bequest.

1982 Socialists under Felipe González win parliamentary elections.

1983 Madrid obtains autonomous region status.

1985 Spain legalises abortion.

1986 Spain joins the European Community (later the European Union), a process completed in 1992. A referendum endorses membership of NATO.

1992 Madrid is European Cultural Capital of Europe. The Thyssen-Bornemisza art collection goes on public view in the restored Palacio de Villahermosa on the Paseo del Prado. A high-speed rail link opens between Madrid and Seville.

1996 Felipe González loses power to conservative José María Aznar.

1999 Celebrations to commemorate the 400th birthday of the Spanish painter, Diego Rodriguez de Silva Velázquez (1599–1660).

2000 José María Aznar's right-wing Partido Popular wins an overall majority in the March general election.

VITALICIO
METROPOLIS

Aparcamientos Públicos
Sevilla

Jardines Sabatini
Jardines Cabo Noval
Plaza de Oriente
Palacio Real
Plaza de la Armería
Calle de Bailén
C. de la Bola
Cuesta Sto Domingo
Cost. los Angeles
Puerta del Callao
Callao
Gran Vía
Calle de Abada
Calle del Carmen
Calle de Preciados
Plaza San Martín
Plaza Isabel
Opera
C. del Arenal
Calle Mesonero
Sol
Puerta
Plaza Ramales
C. Santiago
Plaza Herradores
C. Bordadores
Calle Mayor
C. de Postas
Casa de Correos
C. San Nicolás
Casa de la Villa
Pl. de la Villa
Casa y Torre de los Lujanes
Casa de Cisneros
Cava S. Miguel
Plaza Mayor
C. Esparteros
Pl. Sta. Cruz
C. de la Paz
C. de la Bolsa
Calle del Sacramento
C. Pasa
C. Cuchilleros
Calle de Segovia
Calle Concepción Jerónima
San Pedro el Viejo
C. del Nuncio
Pl. Paja
Capilla del Obispo
C. del Almendro
C. de la Colegiata
San Isidro Labrador
C. Doctor Cortezo
Museo Casa de San Isidro
C. de la Cava Baja
C. de la Cava Alta
C. de la Redondilla
Cost. S. Andrés
Iglesia de San Andrés
Pl. San Andrés
Pl. Tirso de Molina
Calle Don Pedro
Pl. del Humilladero
Calle Duque de Alba
Taberna de Antonio Sánchez
Basílica de San Francisco el Grande
Carrera S. Francisco
Pl. de S. Francisco
C. Tabernillas
C. Humilladero
Mercado de la Cebada
Pl. de la Cebada
La Latina
C. Juanelo
Pl. de Cascorro
C. de la Ruda
C. Encomienda
C. Abades
Iglesia San Cayetano
Oso
Calle de Mesón
C. Mediodía Grande
Calle de Toledo
C. del Aguila
de Calatrava
Pl. Gral. Vara del Rey
C. San Cayetano
C. Cabestreros
Calle de Embajadores
Calle Arganzuela
C. del Carnero
C. Carlos Arniches
C. de Rodas
Calle Mira el Sol
Calle del Casino
Ribera de Curtidores
Gran Vía San Francisco
Ronda de Segovia
Pta. de Toledo
Puerta de Toledo
Ronda de Toledo
Po. de los Pontones
Paseo de los Olmos
Calle del Gasómetro
Calle Soria
Paseo de las Acacias
N
ROUTES 1, 4 & 5
0
200 m
56 Puente de Toledo,
57 Cementerio de San Isidro

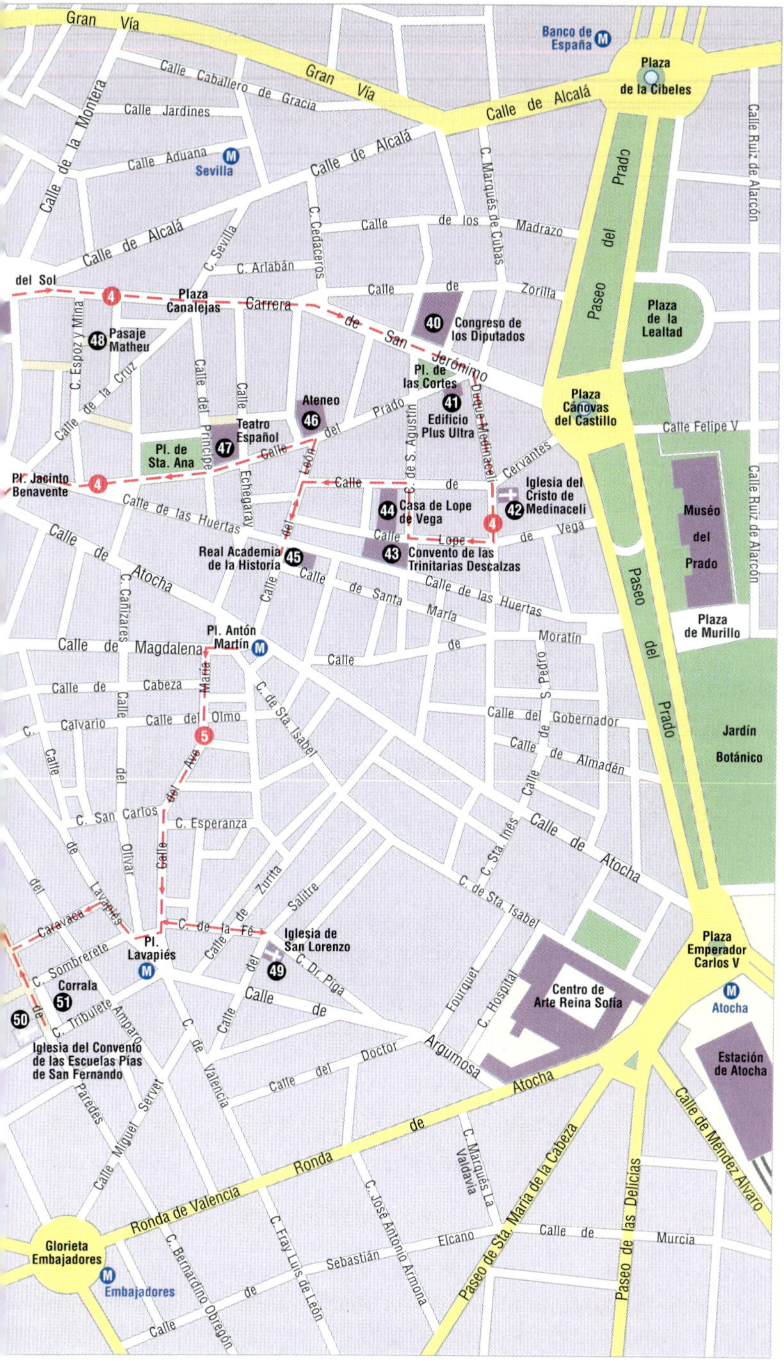
Gran Vía
Gran Vía
Calle Caballero de Gracia
Calle Jardines
Calle de la Montera
Calle Aduana
Sevilla
Calle de Alcalá
Calle de Alcalá
Calle de Alcalá
Banco de España
Plaza de la Cibeles
Paseo del Prado
Calle Ruiz de Alarcón
C. Marqués de Cubas
Calle de los Madrazo
C. Cedaceros
C. Sevilla
C. Arlabán
del Sol
Plaza Canalejas
Carrera de San Jerónimo
Calle de Zorrilla
40 Congreso de los Diputados
Plaza de la Lealtad
48 Pasaje Matheu
C. Espoz y Mina
Calle de la Cruz
Calle del Príncipe
Calle Echegaray
Pl. de las Cortes
41 Edificio Plus Ultra
Plaza Cánovas del Castillo
Calle Felipe V
Ateneo 46
Teatro Español 47
Calle del Prado
Pl. de Sta. Ana
Calle del León
C. de S. Agustín
Duque Medinaceli
Cervantes
Pl. Jacinto Benavente
Calle de las Huertas
Iglesia del Cristo de Medinaceli 42
44 Casa de Lope de Vega
Calle de Lope de Vega
43 Convento de las Trinitarias Descalzas
Museo del Prado
Real Academia de la Historia 45
Calle de Atocha
C. Cañizares
Calle de Santa María
Calle de las Huertas
Calle de Moratín
Plaza de Murillo
Calle de Magdalena
Pl. Antón Martín
Calle de Cabeza
Calle del Olmo
Calle del Ave María
C. de Sta. Isabel
C. San Pedro
Calle del Gobernador
Calle de Almadén
Jardín Botánico
C. Calvario
Calle del Olivar
C. San Carlos
C. Esperanza
Calle de Lavapiés
Calle de Zurita
Salitre
C. Sta. Inés
C. de Sta. Isabel
Calle de Atocha
Caravaca
C. de la Fé
Pl. Lavapiés
C. Sombrerete
Iglesia de San Lorenzo 49
C. Dr. Piga
Calle del Amparo
Corrala 51
50
C. Tribulete
Iglesia del Convento de las Escuelas Pías de San Fernando
Calle de Argumosa
Fourquet
C. Hospital
Centro de Arte Reina Sofía
Plaza Emperador Carlos V
Atocha
Estación de Atocha
Calle del Doctor
C. de Valencia
Paredes
Calle Miguel Servet
Ronda de Atocha
Ronda de Valencia
C. Marqués La Valdavia
C. José Antonio Armona
Paseo de Sta. María de la Cabeza
Paseo de las Delicias
Calle de Méndez Álvaro
Calle de Murcia
Calle de Sebastián Elcano
Glorieta Embajadores
Embajadores
C. Bernardino Obregón
C. Fray Luis de León
Calle de

Puerta del Sol by night, with Carlos III on horseback

Preceding pages: Calle de Alcalá

Madrid's heraldic symbol on Calle del Carmen

Route 1

The historic core

Puerta del Sol – Plaza Mayor – Plaza de la Villa – Basilica de San Francisco el Grande – San Isidro Labrador
See map on page 18

The Morería, the Moorish quarter, is all that remains of Madrid's original Arab settlement. There may not be much to see there now but it is still well worth making the journey back in time through the oldest quarter of the city. Its narrow alleys and squares, still retaining a quiet, almost rural atmosphere, bear the names of long-gone guilds and markets. The classic beauty of the Plaza Mayor survives intact from a later period in Madrid's history, the Habsburg years, while the bustling Puerta del Sol is not just a focal point for three Metro lines, it is also where all Spanish roads converge. The perfect way to conclude this first tour would be a visit to one of the many Old Castilian restaurants along the *cavas*, once the moats for the medieval castle.

The ★ **Puerta del Sol** (Metro Sol) is the busy centre of old Madrid. The name of the square is derived from a former town gate adorned with a sun symbol that served as the eastern entrance to the historic Old Town. The normally congested semi-circle, lined by classical facades from the 19th century, has witnessed many important national dramas – among them the bloody rebellion against Napoleon's invading troops of 2 May 1808, the assassination of prime minister José Canalejas Méndez in 1912, the declaration of the Second Republic in 1931 and General Franco's assumption of power in 1939.

The building on the south side, **Casa de Correos ❶**, was built in 1768 as the main post office, but later housed the Ministry of the Interior, and under Franco was used by the state security services and contained a torture chamber. It is now used as the administrative headquarters of the regional government, the *Comunidad de Madrid*. Its ornate clock tower, dating from 1865, had to be renewed in 1996 because of woodworm. Every year the clock is the focal point for the whole of Spain. On New Year's Eve, to bring good luck during the year ahead, practically every Spaniard follows the clock's 12 strokes live on TV or radio, swallowing one grape *(uvas de la suerte)* for each stroke. A plaque cut into a kerbstone in front of the building marks the point from which all distances to Madrid are measured.

Three prominent statues adorn the middle and north side of Puerta del Sol. The figure on a horse is Carlos III, responsible for such important edifices as the Prado and the Puerta de Alcalá. **La Mariblanca** is the name given to the replica of a graceful Venus figure, which once towered above a famous Baroque fountain. The original is now in the Museo Municipal.

It was not until 1967 that the animal that features on the city's coat-of-arms was commemorated by the erection of the monument on Calle del Carmen. The bronze bear can be seen reaching for the fruit of the wild strawberry tree. Another important symbol for Madrid visible from the square is the illuminated advertisement for Tío Pepe sherry, now an established part of the city's cultural heritage. It is the only one of its kind to be allowed in such a prominent position.

The best place to sit and watch goings-on in the square is the first floor of the traditional **La Mallorquina** café.

Felipe III on horseback and Plaza Mayor

Throughout the Spanish-speaking world, from Andalusia to Galicia, from Mexico to Peru, Madrid's ★★ **Plaza Mayor** is the model for public events and gatherings. Once an uneven expanse of land outside the city walls, used mainly as a market, it was laid out in its present form between 1617 and 1620 at the behest of Felipe III, who sits astride his steed at the centre of the square. It was rebuilt by Juan de Villanueva after a serious fire in 1790.

The square may seem peaceful enough these days, but it has not always been so. Until the 19th century, the plaza was the venue for bullfights, riding tournaments and executions. Now concerts and theatre performances are staged here during the *Verano de la Villa*. On Sunday the plaza resumes its market character when the shady arcades become a trading post for stamp and coin collectors.

Calle Mayor, lined by many long-established shops, runs westwards. You can quickly get through to **Plaza Mayor** via Calle Esparteros (Basketweavers' Street) and

Plaza Mayor: facade detail

Calle Postas or one of the passages further on to the left. Architecturally, the overall effect of what is probably the finest square in central Spain perfectly reflects the Spanish Renaissance. With its unified facades and matching heights, the square radiates a sober elegance. The pointed towers on the oldest building, the **Casa de la Panadería** (1672), are reminiscent of the monasterial palace of El Escorial. On important state occasions the Habsburg dignitaries would have looked down on events from the central balcony of what was once the city's bread and grain reserve. The pseudo-Baroque frescoes were the work of the painter Carlos Franco in 1992.

Located in the building opposite, the **Casa de Carnicería**, formerly the town abattoir, is the municipal tourist office. At the rear of the plaza, the sloping Cava San Miguel follows the course of the moat, which once boosted the town's fortifications. Tourist restaurants occupy the vaults of the 18th-century houses.

Stalls in the glass and iron, single-level **Mercado de San Miguel**, built in the early 20th century, overflow with fresh fare.

Plaza de la Villa

The market for Moorish Madrid (Arabic: *zoco*) was situated a little further on by the ★ **Plaza de la Villa**, the town hall square. **Casa de la Villa** ❷, a baroque structure with pointed towers (1644), is where today's city council meets. Juan de Villanueva worked on the facade overlooking the Calle Mayor between 1771 and 1787. Contributing to the splendour of the rooms inside are an impressive collection of Gobelin tapestries, crystal chandeliers and paintings. Fine mahogany furniture and a fresco by Vicente Palomino (17th century) are the most striking features in the council chamber.

On the south side of the square, linked to the town hall by an archway, is the **Casa de Cisneros** ❸, a palace built in 1537 and named after the architect, a nephew of the great Cardinal Francisco Ximénez de Cisneros. Now the residence of the mayor of Madrid, it is the Plateresque facade in Calle del Sacramento which attracts most attention. The tapestries (dating from the 15th/16th centuries) and the town hall are open to the public on Monday between 5 and 6pm.

Opposite the town hall stands **Casa y Torre de los Lujanes** ❹. Dating from the 15th century, it is Madrid's oldest public building. The horseshoe arches on the tower, typical elements of Mudéjar style, are mirrored in the portal of the municipal newspaper archives next door. The statue in the middle of the square honours Admiral Álvaro de Bazán, who died in Lisbon in 1588 shortly before the English sunk his apparently invincible Armada.

To reach the heart of the Morería quarter, take Calle

Cordón. The busy Calle de Segovia was once a tributary of the Manzanares river, beside which Madrid's first nomadic settlers camped. On the other side rises the medieval brick tower of **San Pedro el Viejo** ❺ (1354), a church thought to have been built on the site of the Arab mosque *(mezquita)*.

Following the rising Costanilla de San Pedro southwards, you will soon find on the right-hand side two squares, **Plaza San Andrés** and **Plaza de los Carros**. In the inner courtyard of the **Museo Casa de San Isidro** ❻ (Tuesday to Friday 10am–1pm, 4–7pm) stands a fountain often associated with a miracle. According to legend, the son of the Madrid's patron saint fell into the water and drowned, but was brought back to life by the power of prayer. San Isidro himself, originally buried in the domed **Iglesia de San Andrés** ❼ (17th century) next door, was later moved to Colegiata San Isidro *(see page 24)*. At the rear in Calle San Andrés is the only Gothic Church in Madrid, **Capilla del Obispo** ❽ (1535). It houses an impressive Plateresque high altar by Francisco Giralte (closed for renovation until further notice).

The atmospheric **Plaza de la Paja** was during the Middle Ages the market for cattle feed and straw (Spanish: *paja*). Further south lie three interlinked squares. As the name suggests, Plaza Puerta de Moros recalls the former Moorish town gate which once stood here. Plaza de la Cebada (Barley Square) was the centre for the sale of cereals. A stroll around the large **Mercado de la Cebada** will almost certainly whet your appetite. Finally, off the Plaza del Humilladero, Carrera de San Francisco leads up to the ★ **Basílica de San Francisco el Grande** ❾ (Tuesday to Saturday 11am–12.30pm, 4–7pm, summer 5–8pm).

According to legend, the basilica is built on the site of a hermitage where St Francis of Assisi stayed during a pil-

Basílica de San Francisco and Iglesia de San Andrés

grimage to Spain.The classical facade of this huge domed structure (1774) was the work of Francisco Sabatini. The gloomy interior suffered badly during the Civil War, and since the 1970s no funds have been available to renovate the crumbling structure so it has had to be supported by scaffolding.

Guardia Civil officer

It is nevertheless worth taking the half-hour tour (only in Spanish) as the art collection includes some important pieces, such as those by Zurbarán and Sánchez Coello. An early Goya, the *Sermon of St Bernardino de Siena* (1780), adorns one of the six chapels.

As the *Panteón Nacional*, San Francisco contains the last remains of some famous Madrid architects, e.g. Ventura Rodríguez and Juan de Villanueva.

If you are feeling like a bite to eat, then you are sure to find something to suit you on one of the two parallel roads, formerly moats, Cava Baja and Cava Alta. Several traditional restaurants along **Cava Baja** serve Castilian roasts dishes. **Casa Lucio** (No. 35), **La Chata** (No. 24) with some fine old-style tiling and **Julián de Tolosa** (No.18) with its attractive vaulting are among the most popular spots. Castilian roast lamb is the speciality at **Posada de la Villa** (all $$).

Liquorice vendor

The twin towers belonging to the Collegiate Church of **San Isidro Labrador** ❿ dominate the junction of Calle de Toledo and Calle de la Colegiata. Built in the 17th century for the Jesuits, it was dedicated to the patron saint of Madrid. When the Jesuits fell out of favour with Carlos III, San Isidro became Madrid's cathedral. But the bishops always regarded the elevation to cathedral of a church in a rather undignified location alongside a row of houses as only a temporary measure.

When La Almudena *(see page 30)* was consecrated in 1993, San Isidro lost its special status. Baroque stylistic features dominate the interior. The remains of the saintly farmhand, who lived between 1080 and 1172, are kept in a silver urn close to the main altar.

When returning to Puerta del Sol, follow Calle Cuchilleros and pass Madrid's oldest restaurant, **El Sobrino del Botín** ($$), which has been serving traditional Castilian fare since 1725.

On the left-hand side, hidden between narrow alleyways, are two picturesque Old Town squares: the shady **Plaza del Conde de Barajas** ⓫, a venue for a small art market on Sundays, and the **Plaza del Conde de Miranda** together with the 17th-century Las Carboneras convent (No. 3) where the nuns sell home-made pastries through the gateway window.

Pass the attractive **Arco de Cuchilleros**, a staircase up to the Plaza Mayor, and you will return to Calle Mayor.

Palacio Real

Route 2

From the Royal Palace to the University

Monasterio de las Descalzas Reales – Palacio Real – Museo Cerralbo –Ermita de San Antonio de la Florida – Moncloa – Casa de Campo *See map on page 26*

Just how closely political power, religion and art are interwoven in the history of Spain will become clear on this tour. In royal monasteries the illegitimate daughters of the Habsburgs found a home that suited their station in life. The Bourbons filled the chambers in the Palacio Real with countless works of art and the cultivated Marqués de Cerralbo did likewise in his private palace.

By Plaza de España, General Franco satisfied his delusions of grandeur by building Spain's first skyscraper – behind the backs of Don Quixote and Sancho Panza. Art-lovers simply must view the unique Goya frescoes in the Ermita de San Antonio.

Start out from the Puerta del Sol and initially take the traffic-free Calle Preciados shopping street northwards, before turning left into the narrow Callejón Preciados by the Corte Inglés department store. The ★ **Monasterio de las Descalzas Reales** ⓬ is by the Plaza de Descalzas (Tuesday to Saturday 10.30am–12.30pm, 4–5.30pm, Friday morning only, Sunday/public holidays 11am–1.30pm; guided tours in Spanish; free admission on Wednesday).

Doña Juana, a daughter of Carlos V, converted this Renaissance palace into a convent in 1554. Only women from the upper echelons of the ruling Habsburg family, including many widows and illegitimate daughters, retreated behind these walls to find solace away from secular life. The close link with the monarchy was never broken, so that these 'Royal Barefoot Sisters' could enjoy a

Priest on walkabout

lifestyle which matched their standing. On display in the staircase, which leads to the upper gallery of the cloister, is a magnificent collection of frescoes, while in the gallery itself is a series of finely-decorated chapels. In the main chancel lie the remains of the most celebrated nun, Empress Maria of Austria, a sister of the convent's founder. A 14-piece collection of tapestries based on cartoons by Rubens adorn the former dormitory. Works by Rubens, Brueghel the Elder and the Spaniards José de Ribera and Francisco Zurbarán can be seen in the former kitchen. The famous *Tribute Money* by Titian is a replica of the painting in Dresden. Some 26 Franciscan nuns still live in the retreat.

View from the cable car across the Río Mazanares

Depending on the current programme the grand **Sala de las Alhajas** by the neighbouring Plaza San Martín (1870),

View of the cathedral from Las Vistillas

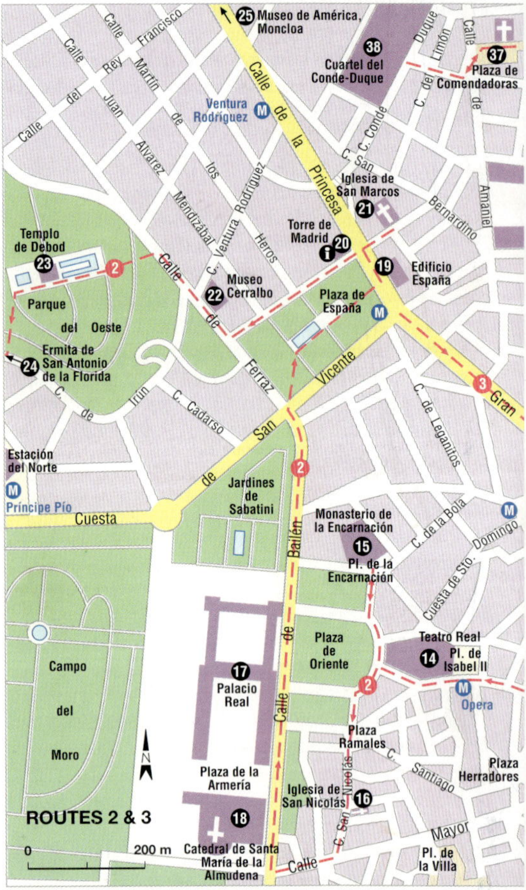

an arts foundation set up by the Caja de Madrid, is usually worth visiting. By the busy Calle del Arenal shopping street stands the **Iglesia de San Ginés ⓭**. Founded in 1358 it was last altered in 1958. In the right-hand chapel *(Capilla del Cristo)* hangs El Greco's *Expulsion of the Moneychangers from the Temple*.

The west end of Calle del Arenal forms Plaza de Isabel II. Overlooking the statue of the queen is the huge facade of the **Teatro Real ⓮**. The Madrid opera has not had a happy career. Work started on the building in 1831, but a shortage of money meant that it was 1850 before its doors finally opened. The hexagonal opera house was closed for decades during the 20th century, with director García Navarro staging the house's first performance in 1997–98.

At Arenal 9 stands the **Palacio de Gaviria**. A seriously rich banker by the name of Manuel Gaviria had this neo-

Teatro Real

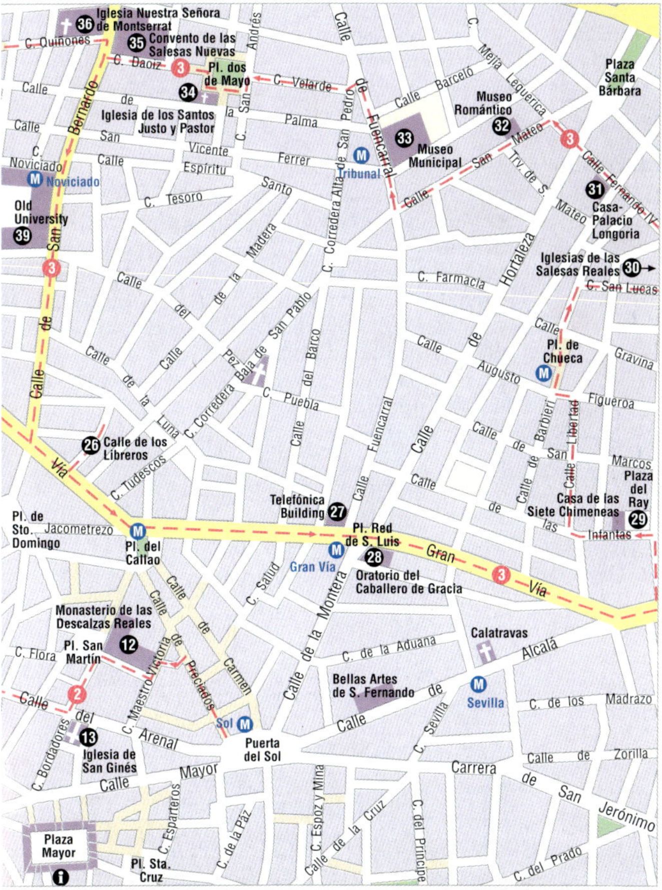

Baroque palace built in the middle of the 19th century. For many years, its ballrooms were frequented by well-to-do Madrid society. A club of the same name continues the dancing traditions *(see page 90)*, but now salsa rhythms and disco sounds resonate from the ornate rooms.

Take Calle de Arrieta to the Plaza de la Encarnación, where, as well as a memorial to the poet Lope de Vega, stands Madrid's second Habsburg convent, ★ **Monasterio de la Encarnación** ⓯ (Wednesday and Saturday 10.30am–12.30pm, 4–5.30pm, Sunday 11am–1.30pm; guided tours in Spanish; free admission on Wednesday). The design for the complex, completed in 1616, was drawn up by the architect responsible for the Plaza Mayor, Juan Gómez de Mora. Founded by Margaret of Austria, the wife of Felipe III, it is still used as a convent. Of special interest inside are the Painting Room, with such works as *John the Baptist* by José de Ribera, and a macabre reliquary chamber, where not only bones and scraps of material from sacred robes are stored, but also a phial of St Pantaloon's dried blood which, according to legend, liquifies each year on 27 July, the saint's feast day. It is an ill omen if the miracle does not take place.

Plaza de Oriente

Between the Opera House and the Royal Palace lies **Plaza de Oriente**, a broad square for which the people of Madrid can thank Joseph Bonaparte. The equestrian statue at its centre immortalising Felipe IV was brought here in the 19th century from the Buen Retiro palace complex. The trusty steed rearing up on its hind legs is by the Italian sculptor, Pietro Tacci. Cast in bronze in 1640, it was at that time a masterpiece of engineering. Statues of Visigoth and Spanish kings from Ataulphus to Fernando VI line the

Statue of Felipe IV in the square

plaza. Situated by Calle de San Nicolás is Madrid's oldest surviving church, **Iglesia de San Nicolás** ⓰. Crowned with a 12th-century Mudéjar-style brick tower, it contains the body of Juan de Herrera, architect of El Escorial.

Built from light grey granite and limestone, the vast ★★ **Palacio Real** ⓱ (Monday to Saturday 9am–6pm, Sunday and public holidays 9am–3pm; October to March, Monday to Saturday 9.30am–5pm, Sunday and public holidays 9am– 2pm; 1-hour guided tour; free admission on Wednesday) was clearly built to impress. Situated in a dominant position overlooking the Río Manzanares, its dimensions alone are stunning (500m/1,650ft along each side). It was built by the Bourbon, Felipe V, with four wings and an inner courtyard, after the Habsburg residence, which shared the same foundations as a Moorish *alcázar*, was burnt to the ground on 24 December, 1734. Giovanni Battista Sacchetti from Piedmont was appointed as chief architect. Externally, the building displays classical Italian features, but in the 2,000-plus rooms it is lavish late Baroque which predominates. As long as no state functions are taking place, the palace is open to visitors (access from Plaza de la Armería).

Guards at the Palacio Real

Heraldic detail

As a rule only 30 to 50 rooms are open at any one time. With such a wealth of magnificent furnishings in dazzling gold brocade, silk and velvet, and walls hung with paintings by masters such as Goya and Velázquez, visitors are sometimes overwhelmed by the extravagant décor.

One of the highlights is the **Salón de Alebarderos** (Hall of the Halberdiers) with its striking ceiling painting *Apotheosis of Aeneas* by Gianbattista Tiepolo (1766) and tapestries woven to designs by Raphael (17th century). In the Throne Room another of Tiepolo's ceiling frescoes glorifies the empire and its rulers. Paintings by the Bohemian master, Anton Raphael Mengs (1728–79), adorn the private apartments of Carlos III, while in the State Dining Room are hundreds of sparkling chandeliers and candelabra. In the small *Salón de las Porcelanas* (Porcelain Room), the walls and ceilings are covered with ceramic tiles from the Fábrica del Buen Retiro.

The collection of armaments, rusty sabres and rifles displayed in the **Real Armería** (Royal Armoury) is one of the largest in Europe, while the dusty **Real Botica** (Royal Pharmacy) and the **Museo de Carruajes** (Carriage Museum) in the Campo de Moro park give some insights into everyday life at the royal court.

The ideal place for refreshments after all the royal pomp and splendour is located a few metres to the south on the other side of the **Viaducto**, a 25-m (80-ft) high bridge over the Moorish quarter and Calle de Segovia. Sit on the terrace of ★ **Las Vistillas**, enjoy a refreshing *granizado* and

Catedral de Santa María

Memorial to Cervantes

Torre de Madrid

admire the view of the cathedral and the Casa de Campo. Alternatively you may feel like a relaxing stroll. If so, you have the choice of the adjoining **Jardines de Sabatini** and the larger **Campo de Moro**, which extends down to the banks of the Río Manzanares (entrance off Paseo de la Virgen del Puerto). Campo de Moro means Field of the Moor and refers to the Almoravid prince, Ali ibn Yusuf, whose troops set up camp here in 1109.

The viewing terrace at Plaza de la Armería affords a magnificent ★ **panoramic view** of the former royal hunting grounds, **Casa de Campo** *(see page 32)*.

Dominating the view from the palace entrance is the new cathedral for the Madrid and Alcalá diocese, **La Catedral de Santa María de la Almudena** ⓲. Displaying a variety of styles including neo-Gothic and classical, it was finally consecrated by the Pope in 1993 more than 100 years after the foundation stone was laid. According to legend, the heroes of the *reconquista* found an image of the patron saint, *La Virgen de la Almudena*, in the walls of the medina and took this as a sign from God. Archaeologists have unearthed remnants of the ramparts on Cuesta de la Vega behind the church.

If you follow Calle Bailén for about 1 kilometre (½ mile) to the north, you will pass on the right hand side the Spanish Senate Building (begun in 1845 but with recent extensions) before taking an underpass to **Plaza de España**. Standing in the middle of a small park with gnarled olive trees is the much-photographed memorial to Cervantes, the result of a sculptors' competition in 1915. The writer appears sitting under a globe with Don Quixote and Sancho Panza riding off towards La Mancha.

The 107-m (350-ft) high **Edificio España** ⓳ was built under General Franco between 1947 and 1953 as a way of demonstrating to the world that Spain was thriving despite his isolationist policies. At the same time opponents of the regime were disappearing into prison cells and poverty was widespread in the provinces. The architects of the red and white colossus, Julián and Joaquín Otamendi, were, they claim, influenced by Madrid Baroque. **Torre de Madrid** ⓴, by the same architects, was the first Spanish skyscraper. Completed in 1957 with air conditioning, it reaches a height of 124m (406ft).

On Calle San Leonardo in the shadow of these concrete giants lies an often-ignored little gem. The **Iglesia de San Marcos** ㉑ is one of the finest works by the Madrid Baroque architect Ventura Rodríguez, who also designed the extravagant altarpiece. The church was built between 1749 and 1753 to commemorate the victory of Felipe V over Archduke Karl of Austria at Almansa, a decisive battle for the Bourbons in the Spanish War of Succession.

Located at Calle Ventura Rodríguez 17 on the northwest corner of Plaza de España, the ★ **Museo Cerralbo** ㉒ (Tuesday to Saturday 9.30am–2.30pm, Sunday 10am–2pm; free admission on Sunday) gives some insight into the lifestyle enjoyed by the Spanish nobility during the 19th century. Don Enrique de Aguilera y Gamboa, Marqués de Cerralbo (1845–1922), was not only the leader of the Conservative Carlist party, but also an archaeologist and a compulsive collector, traveller and scholar. His town house, built in 1883, was bequeathed to the city of Madrid together with thousands of *objets d'art*. The artistic highlight is El Greco's *The Ecstasy of St Francis of Assisi* (in the chapel). No less impressive, however, are works by Titian, Tintoretto and Alonso Cano in the *Galería de Pintura*. Of all the many grand rooms, the ballroom is undoubtedly the finest.

Templo de Debod

Situated on high ground on the other side of Calle de Ferraz stands a monument with an unusual past. The **Templo de Debod** ㉓ comes from southern Egypt and is, without doubt, the oldest structure in the city. Constructed on the banks of the Nile around 200BC in honour of the Egyptian god, Amon, it would have disappeared under floodwater when the Aswan dam was completed. However, the Egyptian government presented it to Spain in 1968 as a gesture of thanks to the Spanish engineers involved in the dam project. The surrounding hills which today form the **Parque del Oeste** witnessed a tragic episode in the history of Madrid. It was here on 3 May 1808 that Napoleon's soldiers massacred the rebellious *madrileños*. The terrible events of that day are documented in one of Goya's most famous paintings *(see page 59)*.

Pass through La Rosaleda rose garden, carry on downhill through the park towards the Río Manzanares and then cross the footbridge over the railway tracks into Príncipe Pío station. To the right on the other side between the railway lines and the river lies the modest chapel of ★ **Ermita de San Antonio de la Florida** ㉔ (Tuesday to Friday 10am–2pm, 4–8pm, Saturday and Sunday 10am–2pm), built in 1798 by Juan de Villanueva. It took Francisco de Goya only five months to complete the magnificent frescoes inside the dome depicting the miracle of San Antonio de Padua. The monk proves the innocence of his father, falsely accused of murder, by successfully raising the victim from the dead. The bright colours, the free composition and the treatment of the theme as a carnival-like scene go way beyond what was expected of sacred art at that time and helped to raise Goya's profile at the vanguard of contemporary art. The mortal remains of the master were moved to the Ermita from Bordeaux in 1919, hence its alternative title, the *Panteón de Goya*.

Faro de Moncloa

Detour to Moncloa

You can either walk northwards for 1.5km (just under 1 mile) along shady Paseo del Pintor Rosales and Paseo de Moret or take the Metro from Argüelles station. Plaza de Moncloa is dominated by the austere **Cuartal del Ejército del Aire**, headquarters of the Spanish air force, a totalitarian-style structure typical of the Franco era. On the other side of the **Arco de la Victoria** (1956), built by the dictator to celebrate his victory over republican forces, towers the futuristic **Faro de Moncloa**. The view from the 92-m (300-ft) high terrace (Tuesday to Sunday 10.30am–1.45pm, 4.30–7.45pm) extends across the city, with the university campus *(Ciudad Universitaria)* and **Palacio de la Moncloa**, the prime minister's residence, below.

The ★ **Museo de América** ㉕ (Tuesday to Saturday 10am–3pm, Sunday 10am–2.30pm; free admission on Sunday) houses a modern-style arrangement of exhibits, most of which were brought back to Europe by the early explorers of the New World. The emphasis is on the culture of Latin America. Prized pieces include the **Treasure of the Quimbayas** from Columbia and the Mayan **Códice Tro-cortesiano** (AD1250–1500) from Mexico.

Boating on Lago Casa de Campo

Across the river to Casa de Campo

The former royal hunting grounds are sometimes described as the city's lungs. On summer weekends, *madrileños* flock in their thousands to the 1,700-hectare (4,000-acre) park to the west of the Río Manzanares (*see* back cover map). Among its attractions are a funfair, a swimming pool, a zoo and an artificial lake with boat hire. The Casa de Campo can be reached via a cable car *(teleférico)* from the Parque de la Montana or explored along a 25-km (16-mile) road network. Day-trippers arrive laden with coolboxes and bottles of wine. The children are left to play, while the grown-ups play cards, *pelota* or badminton, read the Sunday papers or listen to the football commentary on the radio. Some chase around on their mountain-bikes or don their walking shoes. Away from the cable-car station and the car parks, the *meseta* woodland of pines, cork oaks and strawberry trees is remarkably quiet, even though the city skyline seems only a stone's throw away.

That nature suffers from such invasions is only evident the next day. Fifteen attendants are not enough to clear up a weekend's litter. To slow down the soil erosion caused by too many cars, cycles and walkers, the authorities plant 5,000 trees a year. Environmentalists demand restrictions on car use in the park, but their calls remain unheeded.

Cable car from Paseo de Pinto Rosales/Calle Marqués de Urquijo; Metro: Argüelles. Daily 11am–3pm, 4.30–9pm; winter until 6pm. Metro for the zoo and Parque de Atracciones: Batán.

Cable car across the river

Strolling in Plaza de Comendadoras

Route 3

Along the Gran Vía

Calle de los Libros – Plaza de Chueca – Iglesias de las Salesas Reales – Museo Romántico – Plaza del Dos Mayo *See map on page 26*

What is the difference between a city and a world-ranking capital? The answer is quite straightforward: a wide boulevard, ideally one that is both grand and elegant. Madrid's city fathers, certainly not accustomed to doing things by halves, decided in 1910 to cut a swathe through the northern half of the city centre. The Gran Vía was designed on the drawing board by architects with the aim of bringing to the city flair and grandeur on a par with anything seen in Paris or New York.

This thoroughfare has now become fully integrated into the architectural landscape of the city; it has even developed a glossy sheen. Many of the magnificent buildings erected early in the 20th century look almost decorative compared to some of the more recent examples of monumental architecture.

A world of quite different dimensions exists only a few yards from the 'main road'. The intimate aura of old Madrid lives on in the *barrios* of Malasaña and Chueca. Even in the early hours of the morning, the atmosphere in the narrow lanes remains lively as Madrid's legendary all-night party-goers prepare to see in the dawn.

Edificio Metrópolis; just one of many landmarks along the Gran Vía

The western section of Gran Vía between Plaza de España (Metro) and Calle de San Bernardo is lined with faceless multi-storey blocks built during the 1930s and 1940s and of interest more for their size than their beauty. Restaurants, shoe shops and fashion retailers have taken over at street level. **Calle de los Libreros** ㉖ on the north side is a favourite haunt of book collectors. There are several antiquarian booksellers (e.g. La Felipa at no 16) and some shops sell books at discount prices. From **Plaza de Callao**, where Calle Preciados and Calle del Carmen branch off to the south, the scenery changes dramatically. Cinemas like the Callao, Capitol and Palacio de la Música (with 2,000 seats the largest cinema in Spain) attract movie fans to see the latest box office success with hand-painted posters.

Telefónica building

Ornate towers, oriel windows and figures adorn the **Hotel Atlántico** (No. 38), the **Edificio Madrid-París building** (No. 32) and **Casa Matesanz** (No. 27), all of which date from the 1920s. Business premises in the traffic-free Calle Preciados probably pay the highest ground rents in Spain. Air-conditioned department stores such as **Corte Inglés** (Preciados 3), **FNAC** (Preciados 28) and **Galerías Preciados** (Paza del Callao) are welcome refuges during the summer.

The dimensions of the **Telefónica building** ㉗ on Calle de Fuencarral outstrip all its neighbours. It was built for the Spanish telephone company at the end of the 1920s to plans by the American architect, Louis Week, but with a hint of Madrid Baroque to suit Spanish tastes. At that time it was the highest building in Europe (89m/292ft). During the Spanish Civil War republicans and anarchists used it as their headquarters. The **Museo de la Fundación Arte y Tecnología**, Telefónica's arts foundation, keeps a fine collection of works by contemporary Spanish artists, such as Chillida, Tàpies, Gris and Picasso (Fuencarral 1; Tuesday to Friday 10am–2pm, 5–8pm, Saturday and Sunday 10am– 2pm). The inspiration for the tiling on **Edificio La Estrella** (No. 7) is clearly Moorish.

Down at street level

When the building workers finally withdrew from the Gran Vía in the 1950s, the town planners were able to take stock. Some 14 old-town lanes and 311 houses had been demolished and 44 empty sites concreted over. The demolition teams only spared churches, which explains why the boulevard is not perfectly straight. One example is the **Oratorio del Caballero de Gracia** ㉘ (entrance at Calle Caballero de Gracia 5). It was designed in 1799 by Juan de Villanueva and built on the foundations of a 17th-century monastery. The rear facade stands out as an alien among the phalanx of office blocks along Gran Vía.

The bar in the **Museo Chicote** (No. 12) is a good place to stop off for a drink, perhaps an exotic cocktail. During the Spanish Civil War, the writer Ernest Hemingway was a regular guest here.

Try the bar here

A private collection of timepieces in the **Museo del Reloj Grassy** can be viewed during business hours at **Edificio Grassy** (Nos 1–3). Since the 1950s the building has been associated with the high-class jewellery shop that occupies the ground floor. On the corner with Calle de Alcalá stands the **Edificio Metrópolis.** Built in 1905 by Luis Esteve, its dome and winged goddess of war make a photogenic landmark to conclude this stroll along Gran Vía.

Take Calle del Barquillo northwards to find **Plaza del Rey** **29**. The monument at its centre was designed by Mariano Benlliure in 1891 and shows the heroic Teniente Ruiz as, with sword drawn, he gives the order to attack during the uprising against Napoleon on 2 May 1808. Along the west side of the square lies the **Casa de las Siete Chimeneas**, named after its seven chimneys. This Renaissance palace, built in 1577, is now the home of the Spanish Ministry of Culture. A gruesome tale is told about the house; it is said that Felipe II built it for one of his mistresses, who later met a mysterious death. No trace of her body was found and her troubled soul continued to haunt the property. Peace was only restored when, during renovation work, a female skeleton together with coins dating from the time of Felipe II were found in the cellar.

Plaza de Chueca

Calle Libertad, where a number of traditional Madrid restaurants are clustered (e.g. Libertad 8, La Carmencita, Extremadura), leads to the attractive ★ **Plaza de Chueca**, a square named after the famous paso doble composer, Federico Chueca (1846–1908). During the day it is a meeting place for local residents, at night the plaza becomes a popular rendezvous for Madrid's gays and lesbians. If you feel in the mood for a glass of wine, then do try the **Bodega de Ángel Sierra**, which has been in existence since 1908. With its mahogany panelling and old tiles, it is almost a museum piece in itself.

Bodega de Ángel Sierra

Only a few blocks to the northeast is the ★ **Iglesia de las Salesas Reales** **30**. This church stands overlooking the square of the same name. Sometimes referred to as the Iglesia de Santa Bárbara, it was built between 1749 and 1758 for Fernando VI's wife, Bárbara de Bragança, who had made herself very unpopular with the people because of her extravagant tastes. She chose the French Salesian Order to run the church and convent. Very little remained of the monastery after a serious fire in 1915. The reconstruction on **Plaza de la Villa de París** is now used by the Ministry of Justice. Designed by the Parisian architect, François Carlier, the richly-decorated late Baroque interior has clear French influences. Frescoes by González Gutiérrez and paintings by Francesco de Mura have transformed the dome and altar into a Rococo gem, making it a popular venue for weddings. The most extravagant pieces are the tombstones of the royal couple, who unusually chose their own church as their last resting-place. Most kings and queens are buried at El Escorial.

Museo Municipal

On the corner of Calle Fernando VI and Calle Pelayo you will come across one of the rare examples of Spanish Art Nouveau. The **Casa-Palacio Longoria** 31 was built in 1902 by the Catalan, Josep Grasès Riera, for a banker by the name of Longoria. The building with its characteristic flowing forms is now used by the Spanish Writers' Guild.

Travesía de San Mateo crosses Calle de Hortaleza and then joins Calle de San Mateu, where it is worth seeking out the **Museo Romántico** 32 at No. 13 (Tuesday to Saturday 9am–3pm, Sunday and public holidays, 10am–1.45pm; free admission on Sunday). Until 1924 this classical mansion belonged to Marqués de Vega-Inclán, the founder of the Paradores hotel chain. Visitors can admire period furniture, pottery and paintings, mostly from the 19th century, and also Francisco de Goya's *St Gregory the Great* (1794). The former ballroom used to be the haunt of Spanish Romantic poets, actors and Bohemians. There is even the chair on which the poet and founder of the liberal *Ateneo* cultural society *(see page 41)*, Mariano José de Larra, *'El Fígaro'* (1809–37), shot himself after being rejected in love.

Museo Romántico

The **Museo Municipal** 33 in nearby Calle de Fuencarral (Tuesday to Friday 9.30am–8pm, Saturday and Sunday 10am–2pm; free admission on Wednesday and Sunday) is worth a visit if only for its richly decorated baroque portal, designed in 1726 by Pedro de Ribera. The former **Hospicio de San Fernando**, founded in 1674 by Maria of Austria, has since 1929 housed an interesting collection relating to the history of Madrid. Exhibits include countless artefacts, works of art and historic maps and models, all tracing the development of the city from the Stone Age to the present day. Of all the paintings in the museum it is probably Goya's *Alegoría de la Villa de Madrid* (1810) which deserves most attention. The studies used by the writer, Ramón Gómez de la Serna (1888–1963), and the historian Ramón de Mesonero Romanos (1803–82), also founder of the adjoining municipal library, have been recreated here.

On the other side of Calle de Fuencarral lies ★ **Plaza del Dos de Mayo**, the busy centre of the Malasaña artisans' quarter. A simple brick gateway, all that is left of the Monteleón barracks where the rebels held out to the bitter end, serves as a reminder of the bloody uprising of 2 May 1808. The memorial in front of the gateway represents the leader of the resistance movement, Daoiz y Velarde. The *madrileños*, who had fought Napoleon's troops under General Murat with kitchen knives and pitchforks, had no chance. Among the 1,500 civilians who lost their lives in the street battles was a brave young woman by the name of Manuela Malasaña. The quarter now bears her name.

Facade on Plaza del Dos de Mayo

The day's activities on this spacious square are split into two halves. During daylight hours it belongs to the residents of the district but after sunset it is taken over by *punkis, rockeros, girlies* and members of all the other young people's *tribus* (tribes). On summer weekends the squares between Glorieta de Bilbao and Calle San Vicente Ferrer and the surrounding roads are besieged by Madrid's burgeoning youth culture and the whole area becomes an open-air event. But outsiders should take care with their wallets and handbags.

One or two establishments which date from the cultural renaissance of the 1970s and 1980s have survived, for example the **Vía Láctea** (Velarde 18), **Maravillas** (Ferrer 33), **Louie Louie** (La Palma 43) discos and the **Comercial** (Glorieta de Bilbao 7) and **de Ruiz** (Ruiz 11) cafés. The **Kiosko Antonia** bar on the plaza is a popular meeting place for writers, actors and musicians.

Laboratorio Juanse

If you look around you in the Malasaña quarter, you will discover many attractive shop facades with tiled pictures and enamel plates, such as on the corner of San Andrés and San Vicente Ferrer the **Laboratorio Juanse** chemist (since 1892) and **Antigua Huevería**. The latter, formerly an egg shop, is now a restaurant.

On the south side of the plaza by Calle Dos de Mayo stands **Iglesia de los Santos Justo y Pastor** ㉞, also known as Iglesia de las Maravillas (Church of the Miracles). This house of prayer was once part of a Carmelite monastery demolished in the 19th century. Its alternative name, which at times is applied to the whole of the Malasaña district, refers to the apparently miracle-performing Madonna figure on the Baroque high altar.

Iglesia de los Santos Justo y Pastor

A convent survives on the corner of Calle de San

Bernardo and Calle Daoiz. At the **Convento de las Salesas Nuevas** ㉟, dating from 1798, nuns continue to sell home-made pastries. If you would like to sample one, then ring the bell at the entrance to No. 72.

Iglesia Nuestra Señora de Montserrat

On Calle de San Bernardo stands **Iglesia Nuestra Señora de Montserrat** ㊱, once the chapel for a Benedictine abbey. During the 19th century when many monasteries were secularised, the city authorities unceremoniously changed a place of prayer into a penal institution. Until 1920, it was used as **La Galera** women's prison. The main facade with its huge Rococo tower by Pedro de Ribera (1704) looks strangely lopsided as the planned twin tower was never completed.

Calle de Quiñones leads up to the attractive **Plaza de Comendadoras** ㊲. On the right is the large convent of the Order of Santiago. In their church, **Iglesia de Comendadoras de Santiago** (17th century), an image of St James as the killer of Moors *(Santiago matamoros)* serves as a reminder of the important part this order of knights played during the *reconquista*. The colours of the Order of Santiago placed under the dome of the cruciform church bear the names of the historic battles waged against the Moors.

Cuartel del Conde-Duque

Follow Calle de Montserrat as far as the long **Cuartel del Conde-Duque** ㊳ building on the road of the same name. The exercise yards in the barracks, built for Felipe V's Royal Guard between 1717 and 1730 by Pedro de Ribera, have not heard parade ground commands for many years now. The central inner courtyard is used instead for open-air concerts during the summer arts festival, while the spacious accommodation wings house exhibitions (for further information, call 915 885 822) and the new municipal newspaper archive *(Hemeroteca)*.

Palacio de Liria

Ventura Rodríguez designed the Baroque **Palacio de Liria** (entrance Princesa 20) in 1780. The imposing structure set in gardens is the property of the Alba family. A valuable art collection belonging to the family is displayed in sumptuous palace rooms, including works by El Greco, Rembrandt and Velázquez. Visits only by prior appointment. For further information, call 915 475 302.

When making your way back to the Gran Vía you can either follow Calle de la Princesa via Plaza de España or take Calle de San Bernardo past some fine mansions. The assembly for the Comunidad de Madrid meets in the **Old University** ㊴, while in **Palacio Bauer**, built in 1744 for envoys from the Rothschild bank, the Madrid Conservatory trains aspiring musicians and singers (corner of Calle del Pez). **Farmacia Delueze** at No. 39 is a delightful 19th-century chemist's shop.

Sweet delights on Carrera de San Jerónimo

Route 4

Of poets and drinkers

Congreso de los Diputados – Casa de Lope de Vega – Ateneo – Plaza Santa Ana – Los Gabrieles – Viva Madrid *See map on page 18*

El Barrio de los Genios is the popular name for the triangle between Puerta del Sol, the Spanish parliament building and Paseo del Prado. But who are the geniuses who reside in this part of the Old Town? The *madrileños* are certainly not referring to their political masters who assemble in the Cortes. They could be referring to the owners of the many bars and taverns where top-quality *tapas* and wines are served. The Plaza Santa Ana in the heart of Huertas, to give the 'genius quarter' its correct name, is one of the most popular squares with Madrid's late-night revellers, and a closer look at the names of the narrow alleys and lanes around here provides the clue to the 'genius' tag. Many of the 'greats' from the Siglo de Oro, like Cervantes, Lope de Vega, Tirso de Molina, once lived here.

Inside the Lhardy

Set out from Puerta del Sol (Metro) eastwards along **Carrera de San Jerónimo**. One of the more interesting addresses to look out for is the traditional **Lhardy** delicatessen and restaurant at No. 8. Sample a glass of sherry at the bar or better still a clear soup or *caldo* from the silver samovar. You do not have to choose from the sophisticated menu in the elegant restaurant.

The political hub of democratic Spain is located by Plaza de las Cortes. The neoclassical **Congreso de los Diputados** ⓴ (guided tours: Saturday 10.30am–12.30pm; passports must be shown), begun in 1843 by Narciso Pascual y Colomer, houses the assembly hall for the lower

Congreso de los Diputados

chamber. The building is fronted by six Corinthian columns below a marble relief and flanked by two bronze lions cast from cannons captured during the Moroccan war of 1860. Extended in 1994, it closely resembles an ancient temple. The portal beneath the columns is only opened for special occasions at the behest of the king. History was written on 23 February 1981 when Lieutenant Colonel Antonio Tejero of the Civil Guard stepped up on to the podium and started firing wildly as the prelude to a *coup d'état*. His failure was seen as proof that democracy had taken a firm foothold in Spain.

Note the colour-coded seating in the assembly: blue for ministers and red for MPs.

Opposite the parliament building by a grassy plaza, a **bronze statue** by Antonio Solá (1835) honours Cervantes. The view from here along the gentle downhill slope of Carrera de San Jerónimo extends as far as Paseo del Prado, with its Neptune fountain, illuminated at night, and the Iglesia San Jerónimo el Real in the background.

The Palace Hotel

The **Palace Hotel** *(see page 102)* on the corner of Calle del Duque de Medinaceli has been providing every conceivable luxury, often to visiting politicians, since 1913. Even if the room rates are beyond your pocket, it is still worth stepping inside the foyer to admire the magnificent Art Nouveau glass dome. Opposite on the **Edificio Plus Ultra** ❹❶ (1911), a carillon with unusual figures, such as the Duchess of Alba taking her dog for a walk, performs every day at noon and 8pm.

By Plaza de Jesús in Calle del Duque de Medinaceli you will discover not just **La Dolores**, one of the finest and oldest *tapas* bars in the quarter, but also **Iglesia del Cristo de Medinaceli** ❹❷ (1920). On Friday devout Catholics flock here to pay their respects to the statue of a long-haired

Souvenirs of all sizes

Christ above the altar. It was apparently rescued from Morocco during the 16th century after a heroic episode.

To the south of the plaza runs Calle Lope de Vega. It is just one of the oddities of this district that it is not named after the creator of Don Quixote, Miguel de Cervantes, even though he is buried here. The literary hero's last remains lie somewhere in the **Convento de las Trinitarias Descalzas** 43, dating from 1694. There is a plaque, but the exact position of his body is not known. A daughter of Cervantes took the veil with the 'Barefoot Trinitarian Sisters' and the daughter of Lope de Vega was also a nun here. Of special interest are the *churrigueresque* high altar and the paintings by Alonso del Arco and Ximénez Donoso (open at church service times).

Running parallel to Calle Lope de Vega is Calle Cervantes, paradoxically the location for ★ **Casa de Lope de Vega** 44 (Tuesday to Friday 9.30am–2pm, Saturday 10am–1.30pm), where Spain's most successful playwright lived from 1610 to 1635. The two-storey brick house has been converted into a museum. With some original furnishings and an attractive fountain courtyard, it conveys a good impression of everyday life during the 17th century.

Casa de Lope de Vega...

Lope de Vega's life story resembles a turbulent Baroque drama. As a youth he fled from a Jesuit college, at 15 he signed up for the war against the Portuguese and later studied theology at the University of Alcalá de Henares. As a naval recruit he witnessed the defeat of the Spanish Armada in 1588. Back in Madrid he became a secretary and procurer of women for the Duke of Alba, but then took up writing, penning hundreds of plays over 40 years.

When his second wife died, he joined the St John's Order of Knights and was ordained as a priest, even though he had a reputation as a philanderer and frequenter of brothels. In fact he was even banished from Madrid for a time. Yet the public flocked to the courtyard *corrales* to see his popular comedies. In later life Lope de Vega became a doctor of theology and spent his last few years in penitence, whipping himself to death at the age of 72.

...and the nearby bar

Situated on the corner of Calle del Léon and Calle de las Huertas is the **Real Academia de la Historia** 45. Built in early classical style by Juan de Villanueva (1788), it houses the library of the Royal Academy of History, together with 200,000 books and many other important manuscripts.

If you follow the Calle del Léon to the north, you will come to Calle del Prado, a street lined with many *pensiones* and antique shops.

The **Ateneo** 46 at No. 21 plays an important part in the cultural life of Madrid. Founded in 1835, it moved to this address in 1884. Its main function is as an academy, educational centre and literary club. Before the Civil War, liberal intellectuals, progressives, freemasons and independent-minded scientists met here to discuss the arts and politics. Following the Madrid model, many branches opened up in other Spanish cities. Although Franco suppressed liberal thinking, the athenaeum still served as a forum for opposition forces. Traditional debating sessions *(tertulias; see page 74)* are still held in the café and its lectures are open to the public (see daily press for times).

Opening up on the other side of the junction with Calle Echegaray, named after the politician and winner of the Nobel prize for literature of 1904, José Echegaray (1832–1916), is the attractive ★ **Plaza Santa Ana** with a memorial to Calderón (1880) in the middle. The foundation stone for the square was laid in 1610 by José I, otherwise known as Joseph Bonaparte.

The impressive glass facade of the **Reina Victoria** hotel dates from 1919. A popular haunt with bullfighters and fans, it has lost some of its former splendour.

Inside the Viva Madrid

The other end of the plaza is occupied by the **Teatro Español** ㊼. In the 16th century, theatre groups performed in what was then known as the **Corral de Comedias del Príncipe**. The present building was designed in 1802 by Juan de Villanueva. After a series of fires and recent modernisation, the theatre, where mainly classical Spanish dramas are performed, now radiates with fresh colours.

A number of bars nearby have become tourist attractions in their own right: **Cervecería Alemana** (since 1904), **Cervecería Santa Ana**, the **Café Central** jazz club (on nearby Plaza del Ángel) and the fashionable ★**Los Gabrieles** and ★ **Viva Madrid** (Echegaray 17 and Manuel Fernández González 7 respectively).

Tirso de Molina remembered

Manzanilla, the smooth dry sherry from Sanlúcar de Barrameda, is the most popular drink in the Huertas quarter. For the best manzanilla in Madrid, plus delicious olive *tapas*, visit **Taverne La Venencia**, Echegaray 7.It is also worth making the detour to sample some of the *tapas* bars on Calle Espoz y Mina, Calle Victoria and Calle de la Cruz. Restaurants beneath the awning in the narrow **Pasaje Matheu** ㊽ serve *paella* and spicy *patatas bravas*.

Follow Calle de las Huertas to Plaza Jacinto Benavente. This Madrid dramatist (1866–1954) received the Nobel prize for literature in 1922. Passing **Teatro Calderón**, a musical theatre dating from 1920, Calle Doctor Cortezo leads to **Plaza Tirso de Molina**. A memorial remembers the monk and Mercedarian Order missionary, whose *Seducer of Seville* (1617) introduced into literature the hero-villain Don Juan, a libertine whom Tirso derived from popular legends but recreated with originality.

Route 5

Browsing at El Rastro flea market

Madrid with no make-up on

Cine Doré – Plaza de Lavapiés – Iglesia San Cayetano – El Rastro – Puente de Toledo – Cementerio de San Isidro *See map on page 18*

This is a tour through the *barrios bajos*, the low-lying areas to the south of the Old Town. Its name, once in common use, was not a reflection of the quarter's geographical location down by the Río Manzanares, but much more to do with its social composition. Lavapiés might initially seem a rather run-down quarter but behind the rather scruffy façade lies a closely-knit community imbued with a genuine *madrileño* atmosphere. Virtually nowhere else in the capital will outsiders get into conversation with the locals so easily, no other district has so many old-fashioned shops and *bodegas*. Immigrants from north Africa, Latin America and the Orient bring some exotic touches to a quarter that has an almost provincial feel. Added to this contrasting mix is El Rastro, a flea market, where on Sunday everything from pure junk to antiques and colourful cage birds are traded.

News gatherers

The Cine Doré

As soon as you emerge from the **Antón Martín metro station**, you will find yourself among the crowds that throng around the market in the narrow **Pasaje Doré**. Standing out among the fruit and vegetable stalls is the attractive Art Nouveau façade of the ★ **Cine Doré**. This cinema, opened in 1923, is now the home of the **Filmoteca Española**, where a wide range of films are shown in magnificently renovated halls.

Descending steeply to the south from Calle de la Magdalena is Calle del Ave María. It crosses narrow lanes such as Calle del Olmo (Street of Elms) and Calle de Tres Peces (Street of the Three Fish), whose names refer to anecdotes about the neighbourhood. A tale is often told, for example, about Calle de Cabeza (Street of the Head). A well-to-do priest, who once lived here, was the victim of a mugger. To avoid leaving any evidence, the robber cut off the priest's head. Years later, after the murderer had bought a lamb's head at the butcher's, curious neighbours wanted to know what was wrapped in the bloody cloth. Unsuspectingly, the murderer opened it and came face to face with the fixed gaze of the dead priest. Close to madness, the rogue confessed to the murder and soon lost his own head on the executioner's block. Later on, the bundle was examined, only to reveal the lamb's head.

The traditional **Nuevo Café Barbieri** (Ave María 45) is a meeting place for the district's alternative scene.

The name ★ **Plaza de Lavapiés** and the quarter it serves probably derives from the Hebrew. *Avapiés* means something like 'place of the Jews', but where the 'l' came from has never been fully explained. Nothing remains of the Sephardic culture, as in 1492 the Catholic Kings forced all Spanish Jews to either convert to Catholicism or leave the country. The modest **Iglesia de San Lorenzo** ㊾ in Calle de la Fé (Street of Faith) now occupies the spot where the synagogue once stood. Known for many years as the church that served the city's poor, it is also referred to as the **Iglesia de las Pulgas** or Church of Fleas.

Madrid's bear at Licorería El Madroño

To get a better feel for the atmosphere in the quarter, walk a few yards to the north. Greying houses with colourful pot plants, washing hanging on tiny balconies, clearance shops, vegetable stalls and simple bars line the street. The people all know each other and always have time for a quick chat.

Licorería El Madroño in Calle Caravaca sells a liqueur and pastries made from the fruit of the strawberry tree – something of a rarity in modern Madrid.

Corrala mural

There is another unusual sight in Calle Mesón de Parades. The ★ **Iglesia del Convento de las Escuelas Pías de San Fernando** ㊿, a monastery church built in the 18th century, was like many other institutions belonging to the reactionary Catholic Church, plundered by anarchists and burnt to the ground at the beginning of the Spanish Civil War. Franco insisted that the ruins be left to stand as a reminder of 'left-wing dangers'. Surrounding the broad square in front of the shattered walls (with a statue of the Mexican *chotis* composer Agustín Lara) are the tenement blocks typical of the *barrios bajos*. The best example of one of these, ★ **Corrala** ⑤① is to be seen diagonally opposite on the other side of Calle Mesón de Parades. A characteristic feature of these multi-storey flats, built in Andalusian style, are the wooden decks, which provide access to the narrow dwellings. This block was built in 1839 and last renovated in 1979. If you are in Madrid for the summer festival, then you must take the opportunity to watch one of the evocative *zarzuela* performances in La Corrala's courtyard.

Two blocks further north, Calle del Oso leads to the ★ **Iglesia San Cayetano** ㊷ (entrance in Calle de Embajadores). The impressive seven-axis façade was designed by Marcos López and Pedro de Ribera in the 17th century, while the portal with two stylised bell-towers is attributed to José Benito Churriguera – the whole structure is quintessential Madrid High Baroque. Unfortunately, only the outer walls withstood the Civil War; the interior and dome were renovated during the 1960s. San Cayetano, the patron of the Theatine Order church, is also the patron saint of Lavapiés. He is remembered on 7 August when the surrounding streets vibrate with music and dancing. To mark the beginning of the festivities, a procession winds through the quarter, with residents bearing a statue of the saint at the head.

Iglesia San Cayetano

If it is time for food or refreshments, return to Calle Mesón de Parades. Hidden behind No. 13 is one of the oldest and most unusual bars in Madrid, the ★ **Taberna de Antonio Sánchez** ㊸. Opened in 1830, it was initially owned by the picador (the horseman who goads the bull), Colita, but was later taken over by the well-known matador, Antonio Sánchez. When an accident forced him to give up his glorious career in the arena, he devoted himself to his small bar. He lovingly decorated it with bullfighting memorabilia, some of his own pictures and two bulls' heads. Literary figures such as Miguel de Unamuno and Ramón María del Valle-Inclán were regular guests. Nowadays it is not just curious tourists who come to the galvanised bar to sample a fine Valdepeñas or a *rabo de toro* (braised tail of bull) appetiser *(see page 81)*.

El Rastro images

On Sunday until about 3pm, the triangle formed by Calle de Embajadores, Calle de Toledo and Ronda de Toledo throngs with shoppers, browsers and strollers. It is here where ★★ **El Rastro**, Spain's most colourful and most famous flea market, is held. The best starting point for visitors wishing to experience the full spectacle is **Plaza de Cascorro** ㊹. Where now an astonishing range of junk, clothing, books and antiques can, on a good day, attract up to 300,000 visitors, there was during the Middle Ages a district for butchers and tanners. The word *rastro* literally translated means 'trail', i.e. of blood left behind on the streets. However, a second interpretation (*rastrear* = to stumble on something) cannot be ruled out. The tradition of selling second-hand goods of every kind goes back to the 18th century, but do not imagine that you will pick up a genuine Goya for a song, as the 3,000 or so dealers here know their trade. In any event, the range of goods on sale has changed considerably in recent years. Instead of curios and bric-à-brac, many of today's offerings are cheap goods, mainly clothing, CDs, jewellery and toys imported from the Far East. Even so, if you keep your eyes open, you may well pick up a bargain. Tourists must be on their guard against thieves here. Cameras, wallets and handbags are their usual targets.

What may at first glance seem like a chaotic collection of street traders, on closer inspection turns out to be organised in an orderly fashion. You will discover this for yourself, if you follow the main artery, **Ribera de Curtidores**, downhill and explore the small side alleys. Genuine junk is laid out in **Calle Mira el Río Bajo**, while clothes and shoes are offered for sale around **Plaza General Vara del Rey**.

Mercado Puerta de Toledo

Specialists in old furniture and household goods are based in **Calle Carlos Arniches**, while oil paintings of dubious quality – the Spanish seem to go for windmills and blazing-eyed women wearing Carmen costume – are sold in Calle San Cayetano. **Plaza del Campillo del Mundo Nuevo** is the place for bookworms to browse.

A Sunday ritual for many *madrileños* is to breakfast on *churros con chocolate* in one of the many bars beside El Rastro and then to prepare for siesta time with wine and *tapas*. If you cannot make the Sunday market, it is still worth making a tour of the district during the week as many small retailers line Ribera de Curtidores.

There are shops in the former fish market at the southern end of Calle de Toledo which sell antiques in a far more elegant setting, namely the modernised **Mercado Puerta de Toledo**.

The pretentious triumphal arch, **Puerta de Toledo** 55, was intended to celebrate the glorious achievements of Joseph Bonaparte, but because of the long construction period (1812–27), it became instead a blatant symbol for Fernando VII's rule.

Puente de Toledo

If you follow the natural gradient in the direction of the Río Manzanares for about 500m (550yds), you will come across the ★ **Puente de Toledo** 56, a stone bridge (1719–32) which bears the unmistakable imprint of Pedro de Ribera, the master of Madrid Baroque. Nine arches span the river and a city motorway. In between are buttresses forming semi-circular balconies. Lavishly-decorated canopies with coats-of-arms and sculptures of the city's patron saint, San Isidro, and his wife mark the middle of the crossing. In 1830 Javier de Mariategui added the obelisks to both sides. Closed to traffic for years now, the bridge is very popular with strollers on summer evenings. Towering above the right-hand bank of the river is a modern shrine, the black and red **Estadio Vicente Calderón**, where one of the top Madrid teams, Atlético Madrid, play football.

Estadio Vicente Calderón

From the southern bank of the Manzanares river you can either take a 20-minute walk along the rather monotonous Paseo Quince de Mayo footpath or else take a taxi to the ★ **Cementerio de San Isidro** **57**. Dating from 1811, it is Madrid's largest cemetery. The grand mausoleums built to immortalise Madrid's aristocrats often match in pomp and splendour the fine mansions these dignitaries once inhabited. One or two local celebrities occupy tranquil spots, e.g. city historian Ramón de Mesonero Romanos or, in the neighbouring **Cementerio de San Justo**, the poet, Mariano José de Larra, and composer, Federico Chueca. The cemeteries offer fine views over the river and Madrid's western suburbs.

Not far from the cemeteries stands the **Ermita de San Isidro del Campo**, on 15 May each year the destination for pilgrims in exuberant holiday mood. This *romería* is portrayed on some of Goya's paintings. Near the church is a spring, whose waters are said to have miracle-working powers. It was discovered by San Isidro while ploughing the soil.

The best way to return to the Old Town is by taxi, but you might prefer to make an interesting detour via ★ **Puente de Segovia**. The bridge was commissioned around 1580 by Felipe II and built by Juan de Herrera to make access to El Escorial easier. Lope de Vega and other contemporaries liked to poke fun at the sturdy structure (200m/650ft long by 30m/100ft wide). 'Too much bridge for too little river' summed up the popular view.

Puente de Segovia

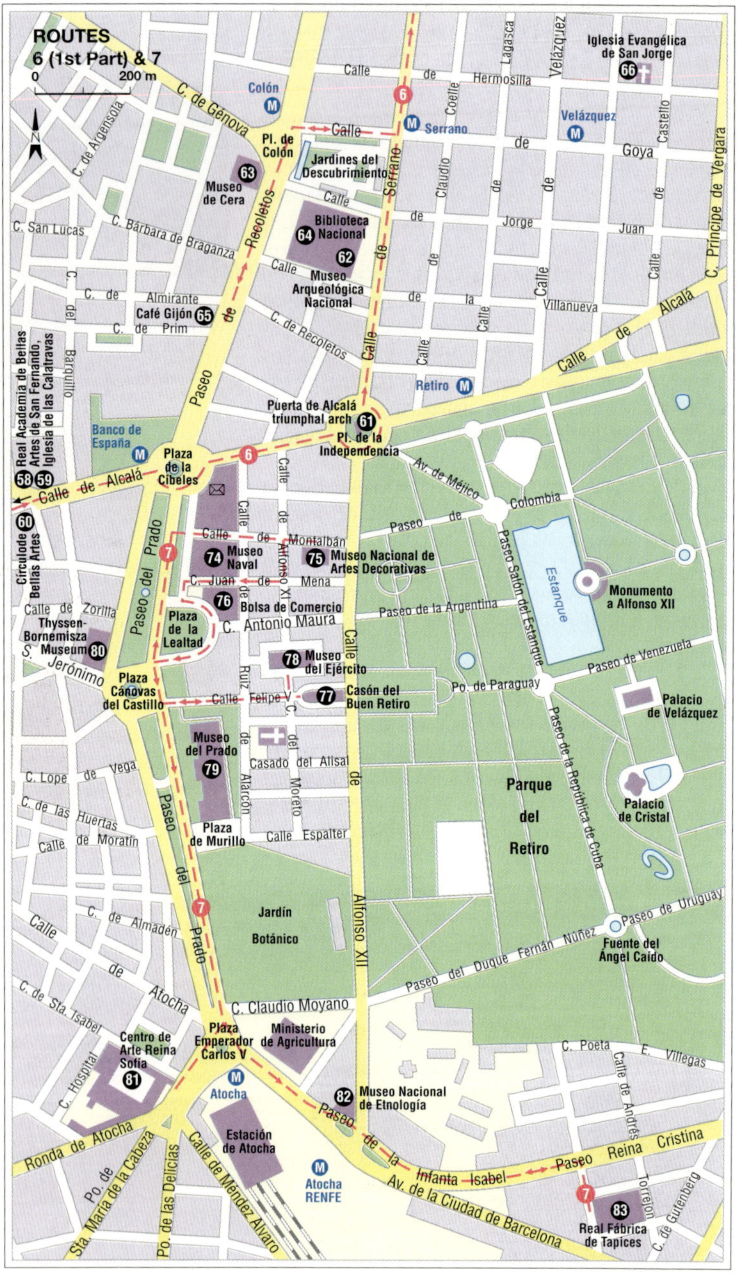
ROUTES
6 (1st Part) & 7
0 200 m
Iglesia Evangélica de San Jorge
Colón
Serrano
Velázquez
Calle de Hermosilla
C. de Génova
Pl. de Colón
Jardines del Descubrimiento
Museo de Cera
Calle de Goya
Biblioteca Nacional
Museo Arqueológica Nacional
C. de Recoletos
Calle de Jorge Juan
Calle de Villanueva
Café Gijón
C. de Almirante
C. de Prim
C. San Lucas
C. Bárbara de Braganza
C. de Argensola
Paseo de Recoletos
Calle de Serrano
Calle de Alcalá
C. Príncipe de Vergara
Retiro
Puerta de Alcalá triumphal arch
Pl. de la Independencia
Banco de España
Plaza de la Cibeles
Real Academia de Bellas Artes de San Fernando, Iglesia de las Calatravas
Círculo de Bellas Artes
Calle de Montalbán
Museo Naval
Museo Nacional de Artes Decorativas
C. Juan de Mena
Bolsa de Comercio
C. Antonio Maura
Plaza de la Lealtad
Thyssen-Bornemisza Museum
Museo del Ejército
Casón del Buen Retiro
Plaza Cánovas del Castillo
Calle Felipe V
Museo del Prado
Plaza de Murillo
Calle Espalter
Av. de Méjico
Paseo de Colombia
Estanque
Monumento a Alfonso XII
Paseo de la Argentina
Paseo de Venezuela
Po. de Paraguay
Palacio de Velázquez
Palacio de Cristal
Parque del Retiro
Fuente del Ángel Caído
Paseo de Uruguay
Paseo del Duque Fernán Núñez
Jardín Botánico
Paseo del Prado
Calle de Alfonso XII
C. Claudio Moyano
Plaza Emperador Carlos V
Ministerio de Agricultura
Centro de Arte Reina Sofía
Museo Nacional de Etnología
Atocha
Estación de Atocha
Atocha RENFE
Paseo de la Infanta Isabel
Paseo Reina Cristina
Av. de la Ciudad de Barcelona
Real Fábrica de Tapices
Ronda de Atocha
Calle de Atocha
Calle de Méndez Alvaro
Po. de las Delicias
Po. de Sta. María de la Cabeza
C. Poeta E. Villegas

Route 6

Where Madrid's smart set live

Real Academia de Bellas Artes – Plaza de la Cibeles Parque del Retiro – Museo Arqueolóligica – Museo Lázaro Galdiano – Museo Sorolla *See map opposite*

One look at a street map of Madrid will be enough to spot the main feature of the Salamanca quarter. Symmetrical residential blocks, a network of roads in a strict chequerboard pattern – quite a contrast to the cramped conditions in the Lavapiés or Morería quarters. Planned on the drawing board in the middle of the 19th century to house the aristocracy and the middle classes, Salamanca has retained its elegance. Designer shops, expensive nightclubs and top-name fashion boutiques have taken over at street level. But art and culture are still very much in favour in the Barrio de Salamanca. The private galleries, auction houses, art foundations and special collections are well worth a tour. If you are in Madrid for the weekend, set aside some time to visit Madrid's classical Retiro Park – on Sunday it is like a fairground.

Parque del Retiro

Archaeological Museum exhibit

As you make your way from the Old Town to the eastern part of the new town, in Calle de Alcalá you will find the ★★ **Real Academia de Bellas Artes de San Fernando** ❺❽ (Tuesday to Friday 9am–7pm, Saturday to Monday 9am–2.30pm; free admission on Sunday), housed in a mansion designed by José Benito Churriguera (1725). Although the Royal Academy of Fine Arts is somewhat eclipsed by the nearby Prado, it can nevertheless count among its treasures some first-class works by Goya, such as his self-portrait of 1815, *Madhouse* and *Burial of the Sardine* (Room 2). Fine paintings of monks by Zurbarán are displayed in Room 3, while in Room 4 hang portraits of Felipe IV and Mariana de Austria by Velázquez. Important works by Rubens and van Dyck can be seen in Room 8, together with the bizarre *Spring Allegory* by the eccentric Milanese artist, Giuseppe Arcimboldo.

Some 400 years of etchings and prints are displayed in the adjoining **Calcografía Nacional** (Tuesday to Friday 10am–7pm, Saturday to Monday 10am–2pm), including the originals for Goya's etchings *Caprichos*, *Desastres de la Guerra*, *Tauromaquia* and *Disparates*.

Further east, squeezed between the smart business premises and banks on Calle de Alcalá, most of which date from the early 20th century, stands **Iglesia de las Calatravas** ❺❾. Originally dating from 1678 and designed by the Augustinian monk, Fray Lorenzo de San Nicolás, this baroque domed church was converted 200 years later to the north Italian Renaissance style. The church had previously been used as a base for the Calatrava Order of Knights, who during the *reconquista* had been fanatical opponents of the infidels. The impressive ★ **Baroque altarpiece** is regarded as one of José Benito Churriguera's finest works.

On the other side of the street, more or less opposite the photogenic **Edificio Metrópolis** *(see page 35)*, look out for the **Círculo de Bellas Artes** ➏⓿. Do not pass it by without stepping inside to admire the café in this magnificent cultural centre (entrance in Calle Marqués de Casa Riera; non-members permitted). Art-lovers and theatregoers met and continue to meet around the marble nude by Moisés Huerta (1910) to exchange ideas. The Círculo's home, built in 1926 by Antonio Palacios, is a typical example of Madrid architecture from this era – imaginative and a little pompous, but not without urbane elegance. The clubrooms are used for public events, e.g. exhibitions (see daily newspapers for details).

Cibeles Fountain

Fountain in Parque del Retiro

Where Calle de Alcalá and the broad Paseo del Prado meet is the often-congested square ★ **Plaza de la Cibeles**. At its centre stands the Cibeles Fountain, designed in the 18th century by Francesco Gutiérrez. Cybele, the Greco-Roman goddess of nature and an ancient symbol of fertility from Asia Minor, is just one of the symbols for Madrid. Several grand buildings form the background for her chariot hauled by two lions.

The giant **Palacio de las Comunicaciones** was completed in 1917 to plans by Antonio Palacios. *Madrileños* refer to it ironically as *Nuestra Señora de las Comunicaciones*. It is not another of Madrid's churches, but the headquarters of Spain's postal service. The impressive neo-Renaissance-style building opposite houses the **Banco de España**. No less extravagant is the **Palacio de Linares**, which was built in the 18th century for an aristocratic family. Since 1992, the 500th anniversary of Christopher Columbus's voyage of discovery, it has housed the Spanish-Latin-American Cultural Institute, *Casa de América*. The elegant rooms and staircase made from the finest Carrara marble are open to the public (Monday to Saturday 11am–2pm, 3–7pm, Sunday 11am–2pm).

On the other side of Plaza de la Cibeles stands the well-proportioned ★ **Puerta de Alcalá triumphal arch** ➏❶. It was created in 1778 by Francisco Sabatini in Carlos III's preferred classical style. To the right of the gateway stands the main entrance to the ★★ **Parque del Retiro**. This 120-hectare (300-acre) oasis in the middle of the city once sur-

rounded Felipe IV's summer residence, of which only a few parts have survived *(see page 56)*. In the tradition of court entertainment from that era, every weekend musicians, magicians, mime artists and puppeteers perform in the park. On summer Sundays, the street theatre performers draw huge crowds. Games of chess and dominoes are played in the shade of old trees, while the city orchestra performs a midday concert in the music pavilion.

Monumento a Alfonso XII

A popular place for sunbathing and relaxing is the **Monumento a Alfonso XII** by the banks of the artificial lake. The semi-circular colonnade with a huge equestrian statue of the king was unveiled in 1922. Two more attractive spots are the 19th-century exhibition halls, **Palacio de Velázquez** and **Palacio de Cristal**. The latter, a graceful glass palace, is now part of the **Centro de Arte Reina Sofía** and is currently being renovated. At the southern end of Paseo República de Cuba is the only monument a town has ever dedicated to the devil. The figure on the **Fuente del Ángel Caído** depicts the expulsion of the fallen angel, Lucifer, from the Garden of Eden – a neo-Baroque rendering by the sculptor, Ricardo Bellver (1885).

Palacio de Velázquez detail

When *madrileños* gather for refreshments in one of the park's open-air cafés, the favoured drinks are *granizado* (crushed ice with lemon syrup) or *horchata de chufas* (a milky drink made with tiger nuts).

If you go north from Puerta de Alcalá (Plaza de la Independencia) along Calle Serrano, after 200m you will reach the ★★ **Museo Arqueológica Nacional** ❻❷ (Tuesday to Saturday 9.30am–8.30pm, Sunday 9.30am– 2.30pm; free admission Saturday from 2.30pm and Sunday).

The collection, established on the instructions of Isabel II, and housed in this building since 1895, consists of many priceless finds from all eras of Iberian history. In the garden to the left of the entrance is a faithful replica of the

Museo Arqueológica Nacional

Replica rock painting from Altamira

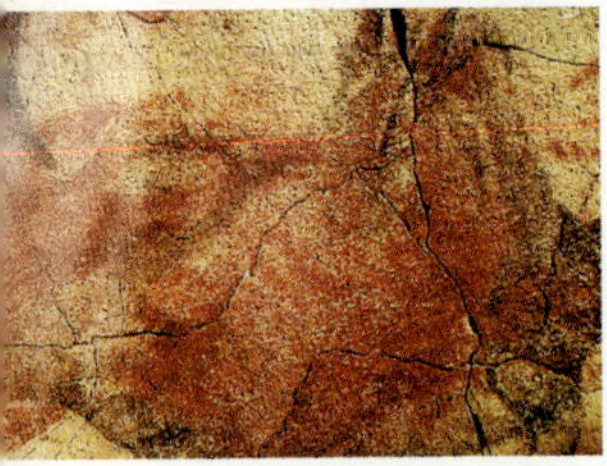

Altamira cave in Cantabria, northern Spain. The walls are covered with rock paintings from this 'Stone Age Sistine Chapel'. Prehistoric exhibits displayed in the basement of the main block document the many cultural links between Spain, North Africa, Greece and other early civilisations from around the Mediterranean basin. The ground floor continues the journey through Spain's past. One highlight of the archaeological collection is the famous Celto-Iberian bust of the Dama de Elche (about 475BC) in Room 20. Researchers are still not sure if the figure with the ornate headwear and inscrutable smile, a high priestess, represents the goddess of death or eternal life. A cavity at the rear of the statue was used for retaining the ashes of dead princes.

Some fine floor mosaics and a sundial from the Cádiz region and dating from the Roman era can be seen in Rooms 21 to 26. The **Treasure of Guarrázar** consists of a Visigoth gold crown, excavated near Toledo during the 19th century (Room 29). Impressive relics, such as a richly decorated arch from the Aljafería Palace in Zaragoza, were left by the Moors, who expelled the Visigoths in the 8th century. The *reconquista* period is represented by an ivory crucifix belonging to the Castilian royal couple, Fernando I and Sanchez (11th century). There are also Romanesque and Gothic altars, column capitals and other pieces of Christian sacred art (Rooms 32 to 35). The rooms in the upper floor document the development of Spanish art from Mudéjar style to late Baroque, but these are being renovated and some sections are closed.

The oldest part of the Salamanca quarter (1864–71) extends along Calle de Serrano from the Archaeological Museum to Calle Don Ramón de la Cruz. The driving force behind the *ensanche*, the planned expansion of the city, was the aristocratic banker and businessman, Marqués José de Salamanca y Mayol. Sadly, his project ended in financial disaster in 1867. Initially, there were not enough takers for his luxury apartments, all of which were fitted with flushing lavatories – a new phenomenon in Madrid at the time. These upmarket residences were all built to the same plan, as can be seen clearly in Calle de Serrano Nos 18 to 62. The architect Carlos Lecumberri arranged the stately rectangular blocks around a garden patio.

Plaza de Colón

The **Jardines del Descubrimiento** at the southeast corner of the **Plaza de Colón** recall Christopher Columbus's voyages of discovery. Four huge stone blocks from the studio of Joaquín Vaquero (1977) represent the caravels in which the explorer set off in 1492 for the Indies. Mounted on a neo-Gothic column (1885), the Genoese aristocrat surveys the square. On its west side, hidden behind a cascade of water, is the **Centro Cultural de la Villa**, where an excellent programme of plays, concerts and exhibitions are staged. The private **Museo de Cera** ❻❸ is modelled on Madame Tussaud's museum of wax figures (daily 10 am–2pm, 4–8.30pm).

Further south by the Paseo the **Biblioteca Nacional** ❻❹ adjoins the Archaeological Museum. The statues at the entrance depict Cervantes, Lope de Vega and Alfonso the Wise. In the ★ **Museo del Libro** next door about 500 of the 3.5 million books, manuscripts and drawings can be viewed interactively on screens. The library possesses the original version of the anonymous epic *Cantar de Mío Cid* (12th century), all of Cervantes' first editions and the first Castilian grammar by Antonio de Nebrija (1492).

Also inseparably linked with Spanish literary history is the ★ **Café Gijón** ❻❺. Situated on the other side of the road, it was opened in 1888. Many of Madrid's intellectuals, from Valle-Inclán to Dalí and Buñuel, met here to exchange ideas. Until his financial ruin, the Marqués de Salamanca lived in the neo-Renaissance palace (1855) opposite. It is now the headquarters of the **Banco Argentaria**.

If you walk northwards from Plaza de Colón past the elegant shop windows on Calle de Serrano, it is worth paying a visit to the **Teatriz** in Calle de Hermosilla. Top designer Philippe Starck was invited to give the former **Teatro Beatriz** at No. 15 a new interior. The restaurant and *tapas* bar now extends across the former stage and the stalls to form a dramatic post-modern complex.

A striking example of the eclectic tastes of the early 20th century can be seen in the Byzantine/Moorish-style **Iglesia Evangélica de San Jorge** ❻❻. Architect Agustín Ortíz de Villajos was given an equally free hand when designing **Iglesia San Andrés de los Flamencos** ❻❼ (1884). The name of the church on Calle Claudio Coello recalls a hostel for Flemish pilgrims (Spanish: *flamencos*), which was situated here during the 17th century. Of particular interest inside is the *St Andrew the Martyr*, which is attributed to Peter Paul Rubens.

Expensive brand names from Chanel to Versace grace Calle de José Ortega y Gasset. **Fundación March** ❻❽ (Calle de Castelló 77) houses a collection of contemporary art in every possible form (changing exhibitions, see daily newspapers for details; Monday to Saturday 10am– 2pm and 5.30–9pm, Sunday 10am–2pm). Explore the garden of this renowned cultural foundation, set up in 1955 by the banker Juan March, and you will encounter sculptures by Eduardo Chillida and Eusebio Sempere. The Belgian Embassy oppo-

Museo de Cera

Iglesia San Andrés de los Flamencos

Sculpture in the open air

Museo Lázaro Galdiano entrance

site occupies one of the quarter's finest mansions, the **Palacio Rafal** (1919). Calle de Juan Bravo will take you back to Calle de Serrano, passing the French neo-Baroque **Palacio Amboage** (1917; now the Italian Embassy) set in a spacious garden.

On Paseo de la Castellana stands the striking **Edificio ABC-Blanco y Negro 69**. Formerly a publishing house and newspaper offices designed in Andalusian style, it has been converted into an attractive shopping centre. One of the shops here, **La Bodega del Alcalde**, sells fine wines from all the grape-growing regions of Spain.

A few yards further north the **Museo de Escultura al Aire Libre 70**, an open-air museum for abstract sculpture, occupies a subway by the busy Paseo de Castellana. Passers-by can admire works by Eduardo Chillida, Julio González, Joan Miró and others.

The ★★ **Museo Lázaro Galdiano 71** at Calle Serrano 122 (Tuesday to Sunday 10am–2pm) is in its own way just as unconventional. Amassed in the four-storey **Palacio Parque Florido**, which the writer and obsessive collector José Lázaro Galdiano built at the end of the 19th century, is a huge collection of art treasures, ranging from clocks, miniatures, fans and jewellery to pottery, guns and furniture. Among the highlights are the paintings on the second floor, including a large *Descent from the Cross* and a series of other works by Goya, a *Rose Miracle* by Zurbarán, the *Seven Deadly Sins* by Hieronymus Bosch, a *Head of Christ* attributed to Leonardo da Vinci, as well as paintings by Murillo, Ribera, El Greco and many more. There are even some works by the English painters, John Constable, Thomas Gainsborough and William Turner.

If you cross Paseo de Castellana at Glorieta de Emilio Castelar, you will find another arts foundation which is worth a visit. In the living rooms and studio belonging to Joaquín Sorolla (1863–1923), the ★ **Museo Sorolla 72** (Calle Gral. Martínez Campos 37; Tuesday to Saturday 10am–3pm, Sunday 10am–2pm; free admission on Sunday) houses some of the Valencian Impressionist's finest works. Sorolla is best known for his beach scenes evoking images of the sea and the Mediterranean sun, in particular women dressed in white, children bathing in the sea, straw hats and sunlight shining through blinds. Sorolla's world, brimming with beautiful pastel tones, extols the simple pleasures of life.

Two blocks to the south, near Rubén Darío metro station, the varied private collection of Guillermo Joaquín de Osma can be viewed in the **Instituto Valencia de Don Juan 73** (Calle de Fortuny 43; viewing only by prior appointment, tel: 913 081 848). The main themes are silk, velvet and brocade textiles, Gobelin tapestries, pottery and arms. There are also some paintings by El Greco.

Break between visits

The Prado

Route 7

The arts triangle

Museo de Artes Decoratives – Prado – Museo Thyssen-Bornemisza – Centro de Arte Reina Sofía – Estación de Atocha – Real Fábrica de Tapices *See map on page 48*

Dedicated art-lovers would have to set aside about a month if they wanted to do justice to the treasures amassed in the museums along Paseo del Prado. The world-famous Museo del Prado alone has more than 2,500 pieces in 120 rooms, through which 1.5 million visitors pass each year. At the beginning of the 1990s the Old Masters such as Goya and El Greco were joined by such modern luminaries as Picasso and Pollock, when the superbly equipped Thyssen-Bornemisza and Reina Sofía museums, only a short walk away, opened. Despite the proximity of such top attractions, do not ignore the area around the museum. Worth a visit here are the finest station in Europe and the oldest tapestry manufacturer in Spain.

Francisco de Goya's 'Self-portrait' in the Prado

During the 17th century under the Habsburgs, Paseo del Prado was a popular meeting place and promenade. At that time, strollers followed the bed of a stream, shaded by meadow trees (*prado* = meadow, pasture). Two bridges served as the link with Buen Retiro palace. Carlos III, justifiably described as Madrid's best mayor, laid the boulevard in its present form in 1781.

Next to the general post office building *(see page 50)* stands the **Cuartel General de la Armada**, headquarters of the Spanish navy. The **Museo Naval** ⓻⓸ here (Tuesday to Sunday 10.30am–1.30pm; entrance C. Montalbán 2) keeps a collection of model ships, nautical instruments, figureheads and old nautical charts, including one by

Christopher Columbus's cartographer, Juan de la Cosa.

Just a few doors to the east, you can experience the full gamut of Spanish art in the ★★ **Museo Nacional de Artes Decorativas** ❼❺ (C. Montalbán 12; Tuesday to Friday 9.30am–3pm, Saturday and Sunday 10am to 2pm; free admission on Sunday). The National Museum of Decorative Arts collection comprises porcelain, glass, jewellery, furniture, leather, textiles and carpets from the 15th to the 19th century, thus providing a comprehensive overview of traditional Spanish domestic culture. One splendid example is the 18th-century kitchen, fully fitted with *azulejos* from the famous Manises pottery school near Valencia.

Rising above the semi-circular **Plaza de la Lealtad** or Loyalty Square is a 29-m (95-ft) high obelisk built in memory of the two officers who died on 2 May 1808, Pedro Velarde and Luis Daoiz. To the northeast of the square, Madrid's brokers go about their daily business in the classical **Bolsa de Comercio** ❼❻ (1893), a replica of the Vienna Stock Exchange, which had opened eight years earlier. Pass the grand **Hotel Ritz** *(see page 101)*, opened in 1910 by Alfonso XIII and used during the Civil War as a field hospital, and then take Calle de Felipe IV to the back of **Casón del Buen Retiro** ❼❼ (Tuesday to Saturday 9am–7pm, Sunday and public holidays 9am–2pm; admission with the Museo del Prado ticket). A leftover from the now long-gone Habsburg palace quarter *(see below)*, the royal ballroom with its collection of 19th-century Spanish art has been an annex for the **Museo del Prado** since 1971. Its classical facade dates from the 17th century, as do Luca Giordano's fine frescoes created at the behest of Felipe IV. Works on display here include paintings by Vicente López, Raimundo de Madrazo, Joaquín Sorolla and other less well-known representatives of Historicism, Romanticism and Impressionism.

Museum visitor

Well-established in the second surviving wing of the Palacio del Buen Retiro, formerly known as the Salón de Reinos, is the **Museo del Ejército** ❼❽ (Tuesday to Sunday 10am–2pm; free admission on Saturday). The military museum's collection includes busts of long-forgotten war heroes, lead soldiers and every kind of •:apon from the halberd to the hand grenade. Of particular interest are swords belonging to Boabdil, the last Moorish ruler in Granada, and the *reconquista* hero, El Cid.

The Casón del Buen Retiro and Salón de Reinos and surrounding park are all that remains of the **Palacio del Buen Retiro**, which was completed in 1633, with a ballroom, theatre, lake and various pleasure gardens added 10 years later. The cultured Habsburg king Felipe IV, who had acceded to the throne in 1621 aged 16, charged his prime minister and favourite, Conde-Duque de Olivares, with creating a better world away from the dirty, narrow passages where his long-suffering subjects lived. Important battles against France, England and Holland had been lost. Catalonia and Portugal were rebelling against Spanish rule and war debts were weighing heavily on the Spanish coffers, but king and aristocracy still wallowed in the baroque fantasies of the Golden Age.

This mentality found expression in court theatre. The king himself loved acting. Nothing was too expensive or sophisticated for the open-air stage. The Italian theatre technician, Cosimo Lotti, worked wonders. Using special devices, he enabled whole fleets to be sunk on the lake, angels and gods to fly through the air, storms and earthquakes to shake the Retiro. Actors were transformed into crystal columns; colourful reefs and waterfalls formed magical backdrops. Felipe's court poet, Pedro Calderón de la Barca, provided the addicted public with the right sort of material. His play *La Vida es Sueño* or *Life is a Dream* depicted the world as an illusion, human existence merely a drama.

This beautiful dream lasted barely a century, as the Bourbons showed little interest in the palace. El Buen Retiro – even Louis XIV, the French king responsible for the Palace of Versailles, was impressed by it – began to decay. Most of the buildings were destroyed during the War of Independence (1808–13).

Queueing at the Prado

The Habsburg dynasty did a great service for the ★★★ **Museo del Prado** ⑲, the unique royal collection of paintings, long before any public picture gallery existed in Madrid. (Open Tuesday to Saturday 9am–7pm, Sunday 9am–2pm; free admission from 2.30pm on Saturday and all day Sunday; tel: 913 302 800, fax: 913 302 856. Please note: a combined ticket for the Prado, Thyssen and Reina Sofía is called a **Paseo del Arte**. It is available from the ticket offices at all three museums.)

Caravaggio's 'David Victorious over Goliath'

Carlos V and his son Felipe II built the first home for their collection when they acquired paintings by Titian and Bosch. Felipe IV, a dedicated patron of the arts, instructed his viceroys and court painter Velázquez to buy top-ranking works from Italy, Flanders and Spain – remarkably, Spanish rulers, contrary to common practice elsewhere, never enriched their art galleries through theft or confiscation. Shortly before his death in 1665, Felipe IV decreed that no part of the collection should ever be sold. This was a principle that even the Bourbon dynasty adhered to. Indeed, after 1701 they added to the collection, but unfortunately more than 500 masterpieces were lost in the serious fire at the Alcázar at Christmas in 1734. Carlos III finally ordered the construction of the Museo del Prado in 1785, although he originally wanted to keep a natural

Brueghel's 'Snowy Landscape'

history collection there. By 1806, work on the museum, under the direction of the architect, Juan de Villanueva, was so well advanced that Napoleon's invading troops requisitioned it as stabling. It was Fernando VII of all people, otherwise an arch-reactionary and anti-intellectual, who opened up the Prado as an art gallery in 1819.

Detail of the 'Haywain' by Hieronymus Bosch

Of the 9,000 paintings, 5,000 drawings and 700 sculptures available to the museum, only about a third of them are permanently on display. The rest of the collection is gathering dust in storerooms and will continue to do so until the Prado is extended. Some 20 new rooms are due to be completed by 2003. The works in the Prado museum are not classified according to any academic theories, but reflect the taste of Spanish monarchs from the 16th to the 19th century. It is not easy to follow a trail through the various rooms, partly because paintings are frequently moved. Holland or England, countries with which Spain has often had fraught relationships, are not well represented, but the number and quality of works by masters such as Titian, Rubens, El Greco, Velázquez and Goya are unsurpassed. If you only have a day, then it is recommended that you concentrate on one of these painters or on the Flemish or Venetian School.

By the northern Goya entrance to the museum (beside the Goya memorial by Mariano Benlliure) is the rotunda with a statue of Carlos V (16th century). Italian painting is represented in the rooms to the left (2 to10) with works by Fra Angelico, Botticelli, Caravaggio, Giorgone and Raphael and the great Venetians, Veronese, Tintoretto and Titian. The latter was a friend of Carlos V – as court painter from 1536 he painted several portraits, including *Carlos V with Hound* and *The Emperor Carlos V at Mühlberg*.

Felipe II liked commissioning *poesías*, mythological

scenes such as *Bacchanal, Salomé, Danae with Nursemaid.* Nude portrayals of the beautiful Danae, painted in Titian's warm shades, were kept under lock and key until 1827 as they were thought to endanger public morals.

The rest of the ground floor is reserved for Spanish masters. José de Ribera, known in Naples where he chose to live as *Lo Spagnoletto* (the little Spaniard), was the chief exponent of the contrasting light and dark style *(tenebrismo)* inspired by Caravaggio. Francisco Zurbarán, the specialist in portraits of monks *(Santiago de Alcalá),* and the Seville painter, Bartolomé Esteban Murillo *(Immaculate Conception),* have a presence here. If you wish to explore the ecstatic world of El Greco *(Christ Carrying the Cross, The Adoration of the Shepherds)*, then spend some time in Rooms 8b, 9b and 10b.

Portrait of the Infanta Margarita by Velázquez

Rooms 11 to 16 provide a summary of the works of Diego Velázquez – the Prado has about a half of all his works. Felipe IV's court painter perfectly portrayed the glittering facade of the Golden Age. In his court scenes *(Las Meniñas, The Family of Felipe IV)*, royalty are shown flanked by dwarves, jesters and court ladies. He was not afraid of emphasising in his portraits and groups the most prominent facial feature of the ruling family, the so-called Habsburg chin. Inbreeding for political and inheritance purposes meant that the unusually large lower jaw was passed down through the generations. But that was only one consequence. The weak-minded Carlos II, the last in the line, suffered for a lifetime from chronic illnesses.

For the highlights of this unique gallery you must visit the southern section of the ground floor (Rooms 19–23, 32–39). In the Goya rooms, containing about 150 of his works, hang such famous masterpieces as *Family of Charles IV* *(see page 73)*, *The Shootings of 3 May 1808*, plus *The Clothed Maja* and *The Naked Maja* – both probably portrayals of the Duchess of Alba, with whom it is said Goya had an affair. Works in Rococo style depicting lively country games, festive scenes and children playing *(The Wine Harvest)* characterise his early period, when he worked on the designs for the Gobelin tapestries in the Real Fábrica de Tapices *(see page 61)*. Goya's darkest side, shown in his later works, can be seen in the basement (Rooms 66 and 67). The 14 *Pinturas Negras* including *Saturn Devouring One of his Sons* once adorned the walls of his country house, Quinta del Sordo or Villa of the Dove. They are the images of a soul tortured by depression.

The basement is dedicated to Flemish painting. One of Felipe II's favourite painters was Hieronymus Bosch – known in Spain as *El Bosco* – who painted surreal fantasies on such subjects as temptation, sin and the Apocalypse. In Room 57 hang Bosch's *Garden of Earthly Delights* and the *Haywain* triptych. Pieces by Van Dyck

(*The Judas Kiss*), Peter Brueghel the Elder (*The Triumph Of Death*) and Peter Paul Rubens (*The Three Graces* and *The Judgement of Paris*) provide other focal points. The Prado possesses only one Rembrandt, *Artemisia*. Works by Albrecht Dürer (*Self-portrait of 1498, Adam and Eve*) and Hans Baldung-Grien (*The Ages of Life*), representative of the German Renaissance, are in Room 54.

Thyssen-Bornemisza Museum

To the west of the Paseo stands the newest addition to Madrid's range of art galleries, the ★★ **Thyssen-Bornemisza Museum** ⑳ (Tuesday to Sunday 10am–7pm).

Opened in 1992, the classical Palacio de Villahermosa (19th century) was converted specially for the purpose by leading architect, Rafael Moneo. With a collection of about 800 paintings, it is one of the largest private art collections in the world. Baron Hans Heinrich Thyssen-Bornemisza gave the collection to Madrid in preference to a number of other European cities, when he considered that Villa Castagnola by Lake Lugano had become too small. He was clearly attracted by the proximity of his prized collection's new home to the Prado, as it filled many of the latter's gaps.

The tour through 700 years of art history begins on the second floor with medieval sacred art, and then moves on to some magnificent Renaissance portraits (Hans Holbein the Elder, Piero della Francesca, Albrecht Dürer), followed by the Italian Baroque and the Spanish *Siglo de Oro* (Titian, Tintoretto, Canaletto, El Greco, de Ribera, Murillo). Some first-class landscapes by a number of French and English Romantics (Antoine Watteau, Gustave Courbet, John Constable) can be seen on the first floor.

Joan Miró's 'Campesino Catálan con Guitarra'

It is difficult to surpass the Impressionist section, which contains works by Auguste Renoir, Claude Monet, Edouard Manet, Edgar Degas, Paul Gauguin and Paul Cézanne. Oskar Kokoschka, Edvard Munch, Emil Nolde, Egon Schiele, Lyonel Feininger, Vasily Kandinsky, Franz Marco, Otto Dix and George Grosz represent Expressionism and the New Realism. In the basement are works by modern painters such as Pablo Picasso, Georges Braque, Juan Gris, Fernand Léger, Joan Miró, Salvador Dalí and René Magritte. Last but not least come Americans artists, including Edward Hopper, Willem de Kooning, Jackson Pollock and Mark Rothko. The catalogue resembles an encyclopaedia of contemporary art.

Jardín Botánico

To the south of Museo del Prado lies the 7-hectare (17-acre) ★ **Jardín Botánico** (daily 9am–6pm; summer until 9pm), founded by the enlightened Carlos III and home to 30,000 different Mediterranean and tropical plants.

The ★★ **Centro de Arte Reina Sofía** ㉑ (Monday, Wednesday to Saturday 10am–9pm, Sunday 10am–

2.30pm; free admission from 2.30pm Saturday and all day Sunday), the third but no less important temple to the arts, is situated by the Paseo del Prado in what was once Madrid's general hospital. It was opened by the Spanish queen in 1988. The glass lifts on the facade – offering a fine panoramic view – and the changing exhibitions of contemporary art recall the Pompidou Centre in Paris, hence the popular name for the arts centre, the Sofidú.

The permanent collection on the first floor represents a cross-section of Spanish modern art. Representative samples of works by José Gutiérrez Solana, Julio González, Salvador Dalí, Joan Miró, Antoni Tàpies are displayed here. But the centrepiece is undoubtedly Pablo Picasso's *Guernica* in Room 7. This huge piece measuring 8m by 3.5m (26ft by 11ft 6in), completed in 1937, depicts the horror of the night when German pilots bombed the small Basque town of Guernica-Lumo. Picasso painted the picture at the request of the Republican government for the Spanish pavilion at the Paris World Exhibition. In his will he decreed that the painting should be hung in Spain only when democratic government had been restored. On what would have been Picasso's 100th birthday, *Guernica* returned to Madrid.

Centro de Arte Reina Sofía

Opposite the museum, on Glorieta del Emperador Carlos V, the train station – ★ **Estación de Atocha** – is a redesign, carried out in 1993 by Rafael Moneo, of a late 19th-century Art Nouveau glass and cast iron construction. The lush palm garden under the vaulting of the main hall is shrouded in a tropical mist created by air humidifiers. It has become a popular meeting place – and not just on cold winter days. Both the old-style *Tren de las Fresas* or Strawberry Train *(see page 96)* and the high-speed AVE to Andalusia leave from here. The colonial-style **Samarkanda** ($) restaurant serves modern Spanish dishes.

Estación de Atocha: mural

Situated beside the imposing Ministerio de Agricultura (1897), the **Museo Nacional de Etnología** ⓲ (Tuesday to Saturday 10am–7.30pm, Sunday until 2pm) recalls the greatness of Spain as a colonial power. The ethnological exhibits originate mainly from Latin America, Equatorial Guinea and the Philippines.

Ethnology Museum

It is worth taking a short detour along Calle Fuenterrabía to visit the **Real Fábrica de Tapices** 83 (Monday to Friday 9am–noon). Felipe V founded the Royal Tapestry Factory in 1721, and Gobelin tapestries and carpets continue to be knotted by hand or woven on looms. The company is still owned by the same Flemish family the Spanish king summoned to Madrid in the 18th century. Much of the company's work today involves restoring the original tapestries, but private commissions are accepted.

Route 8

North to Puerta de Europa

Museo Nacional de Ciencias Naturales – Urbanización AZCA – Torre Picasso – Palacio de Congresos – Puerto de Europa *See map below*

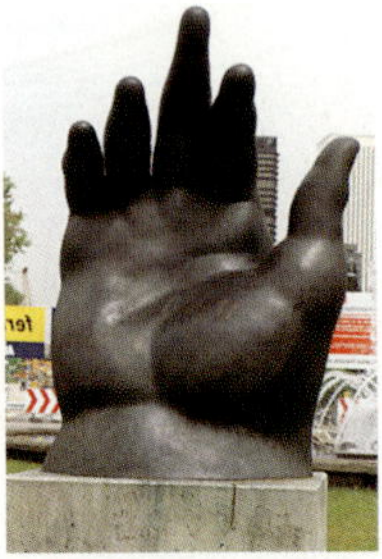

Roadside sculpture on Paseo de la Castellana

The northern section of Paseo de Castellana has the same role as Gran Vía did just under a century ago. This boulevard is the commercial and political billboard for a Spain that has embraced the modern era. Chrome, glass and concrete dominate the Urbanización AZCA, whose skyscrapers are among the most spectacular in Europe.

Paseo de la Castellana, usually shortened to *La Castellana*, is an extension of Paseo del Prado and Paseo de Recoletos – together they bisect the town along a north-south axis. From the Plaza de Colón to the outskirts, the six-lane highway measures 6km (4 miles) and in places is 130m (425ft) wide. Commuters in a hurry, impatient motorcyclists and taxi-drivers regard La Castellana as their private racetrack, unless, as often happens, the thoroughfare is brought to a standstill by congestion.

Until the 19th century, this grand boulevard, itself twice as long as the Champs Elysées in Paris, was nothing more than a dried-up river bed. It became part of the expansion programme in the 1860s. One or two of the palatial town houses from this era can be seen near Plaza Colón, but now most are overshadowed by office blocks. After the war Franco used the Paseo for military parades, renaming it Avenida del Generalísimo. During the 1960s, speculators drove property prices up to dizzying levels, so now only foreign investors, banks and large multinationals can afford to pay the rents in this prestigious location.

The cheapest way to make a sightseeing tour is on the **No. 27 bus** (Atocha–Plaza de Castilla), which follows almost the full length of Paseo de la Castellana. Some sights along La Castellana have already been covered in Route 6 *(see page 49)*, so descriptions here begin to the north of the junction with Calle de Maria de Molina

Until 1932 the granite grey **Nuevos Ministerios** ('New Ministries') complex, which dominates the left-hand side of the road, was a racecourse. This charmless office block was planned during the Second Republic, but

completed in the 1950s. The glazed arcaded facade overlooking the Castellana (1982) and, in front of the building, a sculpture of an outsized hand by Fernando Botero, help to relieve the monotony of these sprawling offices.

Nuevos Ministerios

To the southeast above a memorial to Isabella of Castile is the ★ **Museo Nacional de Ciencias Naturales** (84), the Natural Sciences Museum (Tuesday to Friday 10am–6pm, Saturday 10am–8pm, Sunday 10am–2pm). This grand building, dating from 1887, is fronted by a pleasing neo-Renaissance brick facade. Based around the Royal Natural History Collection founded by Fernando VI, the museum was revived in 1994 after a long period of slumber. Geology, mineralogy, zoology and palaeontology are the main themes, with the dinosaur skeleton proving very popular among visiting school parties. Reckoned to be 1.8 million years old, the bones of *Megatherium americanum* from the late Cenozoic period were found in Argentina in 1788 by the Dominican monk, Manuel Torres.

Museo Nacional de Ciencias Naturales

The ★ **Urbanización AZCA** (Alta Zona de la Castellana) is a symbol for the spectacular economic progress achieved in Spain during the post-war boom years. The architect, Antonio Perpiñá, drew up the plans for this office and shopping quarter as long ago as 1959, but it was another five years before work started on the **Torre Corte Inglés**. The town planners moved traffic beneath the spacious garden and pedestrian esplanade, linked at several levels by office blocks and shopping centres.

The **Torre BBV** (Banco Bilbao-Vizcaya) (85), built between 1974 and 1982, was the most controversial element because the architect, Francisco Javier Saínz de Oiza, chose for the outer skin of the 108-m (354-ft) high complex a steel alloy which oxidised over time into a rusty red colour.

Torre BBV

With 43 floors and a height of 157m (515ft) the ★ **Torre Picasso** 86 is the tallest structure in Madrid. It was built in 1988 by the Japanese architect Minoru Yamasaki, who also designed the New York Trade Center. The air-conditioning and security in this white giant made from glass and aluminium are computer-controlled. None of the 4,700 workers can enter their office without a pass.

Moda Shopping Centre and **Torre Europa** 87, with a clock incorporated into its exterior concrete supports, was designed by Miguel Oriol e Ybarra (1988) and marks the northern edge of the AZCA complex. Despite the ambitious plans, the whole project has clearly not lived up to expectations. It was intended to be a lively meeting place for workers and shoppers, but once the offices have closed at night, the plazas become concrete deserts.

In 1980 the rectangular **Palacio de Congresos** 88 to the north of AZCA was decorated with a giant mural designed by Joan Miró. Opposite rises the enormous concrete bowl of the **Estadio Santiago Bernabéu** 89. Since 1947 this stadium, which holds 105,000 spectators, has been the venue for the many triumphs of Real Madrid football club.

On Plaza de Castilla, directly behind a huge memorial to José Calvo Sotelo, a Republican politician murdered by the Falangists in 1936, stand what are probably the most striking examples of contemporary Madrid architecture, the twin towers of the ★ **Puerta de Europa** 90 (also known as Torres KIO). Designed by the top American architect, Philip Johnson, and his partner, John Burgee, and opened in 1998, the 27-storey high-tech towers, clad in steel and blue glass, lean towards each other at an angle of 15°. Situated at a busy junction of two northbound arteries, the resulting 'triumphal arch' reflects the restoration of Spain's role within a united Europe.

The towers of Puerta de Europa and attendant sculpture

Further Sights

★ Palacio de El Pardo

This palace, a hunting lodge for Castilian kings since the 14th century, is situated in the northwest outskirts. Converted under Carlos III by Francisco Sabatini and later a residence for General Franco, it is now used by guests of the state. It boasts a fine collection of Gobelin tapestries. (Monday to Saturday 10am– 5pm, Sunday 10am– 2pm; free admission on Wednesday; closed during state visits.)

For further information call 91 542 0059. Bus No. 601 (Alacuber) every 15 minutes from Paseo Moret/Calle Princesa; Metro: Moncloa.

★ Fundación Infante de Orleáns

A collection of historic aircraft can be seen in Hanger 2 at the **Cuatro Vientos** aerodrome by National Highway V to Extremadura. A highlight of the collection is the **De Havilland 'Dragon Rapide'** in which Franco flew from the Canary Islands to Spanish Morocco in 1936 in the early stages of the Civil War. On the first Sunday in the month about 20 vintage flying machines built in the 1920s and 1930s take to the air for a fly-past. (Tuesday to Saturday 11am–2pm, air show from 11pm.)

For further information call 913 211 657; bus No. 486 from Embajadores metro station or No. 487 from Aluche.

★ Museo Nacional del Ferrocarril

The now-closed **Antigua Estación de Delicias** is not just for railway enthusiasts. The Parisian engineer, Émile Cachelièvre, built the cast-iron station structure in 1880. On display are locomotives, carriages and models going back 150 years. (Tuesday to Sunday 10am–3pm, free admission on Saturday.) Metro: Delicias.

Parque Tierno Galván

One of Madrid's newest parks, it is named after the popular mayor, Enrique Tierno Galván. Children love the Planetario de Madrid (closed Monday); the **Museo de Ángel Nieto** motorcycling museum is devoted to the world champion racing motorcyclist. Metro: Méndez Alvaro

Monument at Las Ventas

Las Ventas

Murió un torero y nació un ángel, 'a torero died and an angel was born' is the inscription on the sculpture honouring the bullfighter, José Cubero or Yiyo, who died in 1985. Behind it towers the **Plaza de Toros Las Ventas**, a neo-Mudéjar temple for bullfighting fans (1929) with seating for 23,000. The museum, **Museo Taurino**, remembers some of the all-time greats from the world of bullfighting. (Monday to Friday 9.30am–2.30pm.) Metro: Ventas.

Finery in porcelain, Toledo

Excursions

★★ El Escorial

The monasterial palace of **San Lorenzo de El Escorial** *(see also page 71)*, is situated on the exposed southern slopes of the Sierra de Guadarrama (49km/31 miles northwest of Madrid) and dominates the surrounding countryside. Under the direction of Juan Herrera, Felipe II's wish for residential space, studies, a monastery and church in one architecturally harmonious complex was realised with this rather austere Renaissance edifice. At the same time, it was a symbol of the strict national and personal image that Felipe II wished to create, but one which today's visitors find almost chilling. Within the rectangular complex (206m/675ft long and 161m/528ft wide), there are no fewer than 400 rooms and 16 inner courtyards. (Tuesday to Sunday 10am–7pm; winter until 6pm.)

By train: Service C-8a leaves Chamartín every hour. ***By bus:*** Empresa Herranz, Fernández de los Ríos/Isaac Peral. ***Metro:*** Moncloa.

Toledo's Puente de Alcantara

★★★ Toledo

Toledo (pop. 63,500; 71km/44 miles south of Madrid) embodies Spanish history like no other city, whether as a junction of important Roman roads, the capital of the Visigoth empire, an Arab emirate or Castilian seat of government which became a cultural centre in medieval Spain. Set on a rock high above a loop in the Río Tajo, it had all the prerequisites for an invincible fortress. Nowadays the town depends to a large extent on tourism and the souvenir industry, though its famous razor blades are also much in demand.

Armour in the Alcázar

The main square in the labyrinthine Old Town is the Plaza de Zocodover. Start from here and follow the signposts to the imposing ★★ **Cathedral**, where the highlights are the carved reredos (1504) and the magnificent collection of paintings in the *Sacristía* (Goya, Velázquez, El Greco, Bellini). Most of the visionary paintings by Domenico Theotocopoulos – to give El Greco his real name – in the ★★ **Casa Museo de El Greco** originated in Toledan churches. The nearby Mudéjar-style ★★ **Sinagoga del Tránsito** (14th century) bears witness to the great importance of the Jewish community, before it was wiped out by the Inquisition. Another synagogue was converted into the **Santa María la Blanca** in 1405.

The city skyline is dominated not just by the cathedral but also by the rebuilt **Alcázar**. During a 70-day siege by Republican forces in 1936, the fortress, erected on the site of an 11th century Roman castle, was almost completely destroyed.

The best way to avoid the crowds and enjoy the Old Town is to stay overnight.

By train: from Atocha about every two hours. ***By bus:*** from Estación Sur de Autobuses. ***Metro:*** Méndez Alvaro.

Toledo cathedral

The Alcázar fortress

★★ Avila

The main attraction in Spain's highest provincial capital (1,128 m/3,700ft; pop. 48,000; 113km/70 miles from Madrid) is the spectacular ★★ **city wall**. Dating from the 11th century, it is 2,500m (2,730yds) in length and has no fewer than 90 towers and nine gates. The **Convento de Santa Teresa** was built over the birthplace of Teresa of Avila (1515–82), a mystic beatified in 1622. The 12th-century ★★ **cathedral** – the apse is an integral part of the city walls – is worth a visit for its carved choir stalls and the tomb of Bishop Madrigal (1518).

By train: several trains each day from Chamartín and Atocha. ***By bus:*** Empresa Larrea, Paseo de la Florida 11. ***Metro:*** Príncipe Pío.

★★ Segovia

Segovia (pop. 58,000; 88km/55 miles from Madrid) is home to many fine mansions and Romanesque churches, but there are three important tourist attractions: the 728-m (2,388-ft) long and 29-m (95-ft) high ★★ **Roman aqueduct** which dates from the first century and supplied the town's water until the 1960s, the ★★ **cathedral** in Isabelline Gothic and the ★★ **Alcázar**, an extraordinary Castilian fairy-tale castle (daily 10am–7pm; winter until 6pm), with a magnificent view.

About 11km (7 miles) southeast of Segovia, Felipe V built a smaller version of Versailles, the summer palace where he spent his youth. What attracts most visitors to ★ **La Granja de San**

Opposite: Toledo armour

Ildefenso are the Baroque palace gardens with their countless fountains and water features (Monday to Saturday 10am–1.30pm, 3–5pm, Sunday 10am–2pm; summer, daily 10am–6pm).

By train: from Atocha or Chamartín. ***By bus:*** La Sepulvedana from Paseo de la Florida 11. ***Metro:*** Príncipe Pío.

Alcalá de Henares

Cervantes statue

★ Alcalá de Henares

Cardinal Cisneros, father confessor and *éminence grise* at the court of the Catholic Kings, established the Universidad Complutense in Alcalá de Henares (pop. 160,000; 32km/20 miles east of Madrid) in 1498. Most of the original 40 colleges have been destroyed, but the much restored ★ **Colegio Mayor de San Ildefenso** on Plaza de Diego survives. The Renaissance façade and the attractive patios date from between 1537 and 1570.

In the typically Castilian arcades which line Calle Mayor is the **Casa Museo Cervantes**. Billed as the birthplace of Spain's best-known writer, there is no evidence that he was actually born here in 1547, but it is nevertheless a fascinating museum, with a collection of period furniture (Tuesday to Friday 10am–2pm, 4–7pm, Saturday and Sunday 10am–2pm).

The **Hostería del Estudiante** ($$), Colegios 3, tel: 918 880 330, is a tourist attraction in its own right. Castilian cuisine is served in the 16th-century university refectory.

By train: Line C-2 and C-7a from Atocha. ***By bus***: Continental, Avenida de América 34. ***Metro:*** Avenida de América.

★ Aranjuez

Aranjuez (pop. 38,000; 48km/30 miles south of Madrid) was where the Bourbons liked to spend the summer months in their retreat on the banks of the Tajo. The Baroque **Real Palacio de Aranjuez**, with its elegant but playful gardens, follows French designs. The rooms, including the splendid **Sala de Porcelanas**, are open to the public (Tuesday to Sunday 10am – 6pm, 5pm in winter).

By train: Line C-3 every 20 minutes from Atocha; the famous Strawberry Train *(see page 96)*. ***By bus:*** from Estación del Sur. ***Metro:*** Méndez Alvaro.

Aranjuez is often combined with a visit to the small Castilian town of **Chinchón** (45km/28 miles from Madrid). The town is proud of its historic **Plaza Mayor**, used for bullfights since 1502 and surrounded on three sides with three storeys of wooden galleries, and also for its traditional *mesónes* (inns). A famous aniseed brandy, *anisado de Chinchón*, mainly served as a *digestif*, is produced here.

By bus: La Veloz, from Avenida del Meditérraneo 49. ***Metro:*** Conde de Casal.

FCC

Art and Architecture

Opposite:
Puerta de Europa

In contrast to most Castilian towns, the buildings in Madrid – churches, monasteries, palaces and other official buildings – all have a tendency towards the monumental. Romanesque and Gothic, elsewhere in Spain very much a part of the architectural landscape, are not found here. That is not surprising as the city only became a capital in 1561 under Felipe II's rule. A few details remain from the Arab era in the Moorish quarter, e.g. the tower of San Pedro el Viejo (14th century) and the horseshoe-shaped arches on the Casa y Torre de los Lujanes (15th century; *see page 22*), typical of the Muslim-influenced Mudéjar style.

The Italian Renaissance greatly influenced the architectural style of the Habsburg dynasty, the *Madrid de los Austrias*. The monasterial palace of El Escorial, 49km/31 miles northwest of the city, is an austere interpretation of Habsburg ideals. For Felipe II, known for his ascetic lifestyle, this sober palace symbolised orthodox religion and the Counter-Reformation. A huge building, more like a prison than a palace, it was for him the ultimate expression of state and church power. El Escorial's architect, Juan de Herrera (1530–97), perfectly reflected his master's view of the world. The corner towers at El Escorial reappear on many buildings in Madrid's city centre, e.g. the town hall and the arcaded houses by the Plaza Mayor.

Puerta de Alcalá

Madrid city architect, Pedro de Ribera (1683–1742), was the chief exponent of High Baroque, as seen in the Puente de Toledo and the Museo Municipal's opulent portal. José Benito Churriguera (1665–1725), who developed an extravagant but typically Spanish Baroque ornamental style *(Churriguerismo)*, worked in Madrid and produced the altarpiece *(retablo)* in the Iglesia de las Calatravas. The transition from the Baroque to Classical took place under the Bourbons. Francisco Sabatini (1722–97), Carlos III's Italian court architect, designed the Puerta de Alcalá. His colleague, Ventura Rodríguez (1717–85), completed the Royal Palace, while Juan de Villanueva (1739–1811) directed work on the Prado.

After 1880 a dramatic population explosion led to the expansion of the city *(ensanche)* northwards. Characteristic of this phase in the city's growth are the proud town houses in the chequerboard-style Chamberí and Salamanca quarters. To keep in step with other European capitals, in 1910 the city fathers approved the construction of a grand boulevard, the Gran Vía, through the Old Town. It was there and by Calle de Alcalá that many huge office blocks and official buildings were constructed, often copying the style of the early American skyscrapers.

Calle de Alcalá

After the Spanish Civil War, which left nasty scars, mainly in the eastern inner-city area, the totalitarian Franco regime built prestige blocks by Plaza de España (from 1947). The focal point of post-1970s high-tech architecture is Paseo de la Castellana, where contemporary designers such as Francisco Javier Saínz de Oiza, Minoru Yamasaki (Zona AZCA; *see page 63)* and Philip Johnson (Puerta de Europa; *see page 64)* have created bold glass and steel structures. A highly successful post-modern project was the renovation of the Art Nouveau Atocha station (1992) by leading architect, Rafael Moneo *(see page 61)*.

A magnet for world-class painters

El Greco's 'The Trinity'

Since the 16th century many world-ranking artists have lived and worked in Madrid, drawn by royal sponsorship and patrons of the arts. The heyday for Spanish painting of the 16th and 17th centuries is often described as the *Siglo de Oro*, the Golden Age. This was the time when the treasures from the New World enabled Spain to indulge in a display of its wealth. El Greco (1541–1614), born in Crete, was one of the curtain-raisers. Trained in Venice by Titian, he developed his own language of colour and form. His paintings combine Byzantine icon painting and Venetian Mannerism with the Catholic fervour for the Counter-Reformation. Typical of El Greco, who worked mainly in Toledo, are the long faces and bodies and the entranced expression of his subjects. Because the reclusive 'secretary king' Felipe II did not like his expressive style, El Greco did not enjoy great success at the royal court.

Diego Ridriguez de Silva Velázquez (1599–1660) was born in Seville, where he learned his trade. He initially painted in the mystical, religious light and dark style *(tenebrismo)* that was widespread at that time. In 1623, one of Felipe IV's courtiers brought him to Madrid. On two occasions Velázquez travelled to Italy in order to perfect his art. His gift for visually capturing situations and people remains unequalled. The climax of his work must be the brilliantly composed painting of the Infanta Margarita and her entourage known as *Las Meniñas* or Maids of Honour, a theme taken up by Picasso in 1957 and modified.

Goya

While Velázquez enjoyed financial and artistic freedom, his friend Francisco Zurbarán (1598–1664), from Extremadura, was dependent throughout his life on clerical patronage. His main theme was the simple portrayal of monks, staged in the traditional *tenebrismo* style.

One authentic exponent of High Baroque was Claudio Coello (1642–92), whose grandiose works adorn churches, monasteries and palaces in the Madrid area. Luis Meléndez, on the other hand, demonstrated his artistic skill and formal clarity with Spanish genre pieces *(bodegónes)*.

Francisco de Goya y Lucientes (1746–1828) broke new bounds. A farmer's son from Fuendetodos near Zaragoza, he was employed in Madrid as a 17-year-old by the man who was later to be his father-in-law, the court painter, Francisco Bayeu. In 1776 Goya began producing colourful Rococo-style designs for the Royal Tapestry Works *(see page 61)*. He won admiration from aristocratic circles and was eventually given the court office that he yearned for. In 1786 he became court painter to Charles IV. In his heart Goya was committed to the Enlightenment, but he was constantly in conflict with himself, torn between conformity, a concealed rebellious streak and cynicism towards his masters. His portraits of royal dignitaries, clerics and court hangers-on unmasked the rich and powerful in unflattering and uncompromising style *(see below)*. Later on, haunted by the War of Independence and the political turmoil of the 19th century, Goya turned his attention towards social, but mainly fantastical and grotesque, themes. In form and content his satirical etchings such as *The Disasters of War* and his frightening *Pinturas negras* were ahead of their time.

The Valencia Impressionist, Joaquín Sorolla (1863–1923), a painter known for his sunlight effects, worked mainly in Madrid, while Juan Gris (1887–1927) was a master of Cubism and an early companion of Picasso.

Pablo Picasso (1881–1973) was born in Malaga and spent only a few months in the capital. One of his masterpieces, *Guernica* (1937; *see page 61*), has been displayed in Madrid since the restoration of democracy. Works by other exponents of modern Spanish art, e.g. the Madrid Expressionist, José Gutiérrez Solana (1886–1945) and the Catalans, Salvador Dalí, Joan Miró and Antoni Tàpies, are on show in the Centro de Arte Reina Sofía (*see page 60*).

Goya's 'Saturn Devouring one of his Sons' in the Prado

Goya's family portrait

Anyone viewing Goya's *The Family of Charles IV* in the Prado, one of the many portraits the court painter made of the rich and powerful, will wonder at the sheer brazenness of the artist and the tolerance of his subjects. Treachery, ignorance and lack of character exude from the faces of the painter's subjects, who include kings, ministers, bishops, infantas and court sycophants.

In this famous Bourbon family group, Goya portrays a foolish-looking Carlos IV decked out in his royal finery, with an unattractive and bloated, but cunning-looking María Luisa at his side. Their children do not resemble the king, rather Manuel de Godoy (1767–1851), the influential prime minister and the queen's lover. The arrogant boy in blue (far left) is the oldest son of the king, and he later became the despot, Fernando VII. At the rear stands the oldest infanta, María Josefa, Carlos's sister, whose bird-like features Goya captured on canvas several times. Goya himself is immortalised in the shadowy background, eyeing the observer as a silent insider.

Cervantes

Literature

From Cervantes to Cela

The *Siglo de Oro* was also the Golden Age for literature. Miguel de Cervantes y Saavedra (1547–1616) from Alcalá de Henares *(see page 68)* took part in the Battle of Lepanto, where his left hand was mutilated. After that he was abducted by Algerian pirates for five years, before returning to Madrid and hailed as a hero. His *Don Quixote* (1605) was conceived as an ironic reflection on the anachronistic heroic ideal. Together with his feeble donkey, Rosinante, and his pragmatic companion, Sancho Panza, the wistful knight tours Spain in his vain battle against windmills.

Both the Madrid dramatists Félix Lope de Vega (1562–1635) and Pedro Calderón de la Barca (1600–81) turned out a long series of classic Spanish plays. At the heart of their work lie the Christian ethic and the question of justice under absolutist rulers. Tirso de Molina (1584–1648) brought the immortal figure of Don Juan to the literary world. With his *Vida del Buscón Pablos*, Francisco de Quevedo (1580–1645) wrote the most successful picaresque novel of his time.

Jacinto Benavente

At the end of the 19th century, the restoration of the monarchy and the loss of Spain's remaining overseas colonies brought great uncertainty. The disillusioned *Generación de 1898* sought to introduce a spiritual reawakening. Members of this circle of Madrid intellectuals included the novelist Pío Baroja (1872–1956), the poet Antonio Machado (1875–1939), and the dramatists Ramón María del Valle-Inclán (1869–1936) and Jacinto Benavente (1866–1954; Nobel prize winner 1922). They formed discussion groups known as *tertulias*. Named after the early Christian thinker, Tertullian (160-225), these had long been embedded in Madrid's cultural tradition: in the

17th century, educated theatre-goers met in the *Corrala* after the performance to exchange views; and in the next century Liberals and Romantics, such as Mesonero Romanos, Larra, Campoamor and Pérez Galdós, discovered the café as a meeting place. Here they could express views about the absolutist Spanish rulers more privately.

The intellectuals of *Generacíon del 1898* met in the Gijon, Comercial or Lión cafés. The uncrowned king of the *tertulia* during the 1920s was Ramón Gómez de la Serna. Every Saturday at 9pm between 1914 and 1936 the writer held court in the legendary Café de Pombo (formerly on Calle Carretas, near Puerta del Sol). The rules of the game were quite simple: everyone pays for their own drinks; politics and personal matters are taboo.

De la Serna wrote more than 100 books and essays on Madrid. He is best known for his *greguerías*, poetic flashes of inspiration, the sort that can only emerge from a haze of tobacco smoke when the aroma of coffee pervades the air. The painter Gutiérrez Solana was a regular at Don Ramón's table and immortalised the *Tertulia del Pombo* in a famous painting now on display in the Centro de Arte Reina Sofía (*see page 60*).

Also during the 1920s, the avant-garde *Generación de 1927*, grouped around the Andalusian, Federico García Lorca (1898–1936), breathed fresh air into Spain's literary world. While they were studying in Madrid, the surrealist Luis Buñuel and Salvador Dalí sent shock waves through Spain's bourgeoisie with their provocative *Un Chien Andalou* (1928). A native of Madrid, the great writer and philosopher José Ortega y Gasset (1883–1955) shared the preoccupation of his generation with Spain's problems. He founded a number of periodicals including *Revista del Occidente*, and his book *The Revolt of the Masses* (1929) forshadowed the Civil War.

After the Civil War, the *tertulia* provided an opportunity for the few intellectuals who had not emigrated, such as Camilo José Cela (b. 1916), to express themselves, though opponents of Franco would also hold their meetings disguised as bullfighting fans *(peña taurina)*. Cela, whose big-city novel *The Hive* presents a snapshot of everyday life in Madrid in 1942, won a Nobel prize in 1989.

Two of Spain's most read modern authors are Carmen Martín Gaite (b. 1925) – her novels include *At the Spa* and *The Back Room* – and the popular *El País* columnist Rosa Monitor (b. 1951; *The Delta Function*). Javier Marías (b. 1951) won international acclaim recently for his epic *A Heart So White*.

The Spanish still derive considerable pleasure from polished rhetoric and speech-making and the tradition of the *tertulia* is still upheld today in the Café Gijon, Café del Circulo de Bellas Artes and elsewhere in the city.

Centro de Arte Reina Sofia

Javier Marías

Musicians on the Cervantes Monument

Flamenco, chotis and zarzuela

Given the make-up of its population, Madrid is in effect one of Spain's largest Andalusian cities, so it is no surprise that the capital can boast many venues for flamenco dancing. This ancient musical form has its roots in gypsy culture, but with some Berber and Jewish influences.

The heartfelt *cante jondo* is a pure singing style with simple lyrics generally focusing on unrequited love, death, guilt and the fate of those born on the fringes of society. When performing, the singers are fired up by rhythmic clapping and calls from the audience. Guitars, dancing and colourful costumes, introduced only in the 1800s, are now obligatory when performances are staged in the *tablaos*.

Guitars, an important part of the repertoire

One very traditional Madrid art form is *zarzuela*, a form of ballad opera originally performed as amusement for the royal court. Calderón de la Barca was an early exponent who adapted mythological and heroic tales for the stage. This operetta-style musical enjoyed a renaissance during the 19th century. Lyricists such as Pascual Arrietas (1820–91; *Marina*), Francisco Asenja Barbieri (1823–94; *El Barberillo de Lavapiés*) and José Serrano (1873–1941; *Alma de Dios*) filled the opera houses with their folksy tales. The single-act *Género chico* teeming with archetypal *madrileño* characters such as the cocky *manolos* and coquettish *manolas* *(see page 9)* was very popular. *Zarzuela* still appeals today. Open-air performances in Lavapiés *(see page 45)* are always well attended.

It was through zarzuela that the Madrid jig known as the *chotis*, the Scottish polka, became fashionable in the 19th century. It came via Paris to Spain where composers made it their own. *Madrid, Madrid, Madrid*, a *chotis* which you will come across at any popular gathering, is by the Mexican composer, Agustín Lara (1897–1970).

Cinema and other events

Madrid is Spain's answer to Hollywood, not just because of its 132 cinemas, but also because of the *Ciudad de la Imagen* film studios in the suburb of Pozuelos. During the Franco era, several producers and actors, including Antonio Banderas and Victoria Abril, won recognition abroad. Carlos Saura (*Tempo!, 1981; Carmen, 1986)* and Manuel Gutiérrez Aragón (*Demons in the Garden*, 1982) marked the revival of the cinema as a popular medium after the demise of the Franco regime. Life in the 1970s and 1980s was captured on celluloid by autodidact and icon Pedro Almódovar, in his burlesque comedies *Women on the Verge of a Nervous Breakdown* (1988) and *Tie Me Up! Tie me Down!* (1999). At the Cannes Festival he won the director's prize for *All about my Mother* (1999).

In 1994 Fernando Trueba won an Oscar for his extravagant production *Belle Epoque*. After this came the star-studded, Hollywood-style follow-up entitled *Two Much* (1995).

Celluloid heroes and heroines

Events calendar

5 January: Procession of the Three Kings *(Reyes Magos)*.
February: Top-class stars appear during the *Festival del Flamenco*.
Carnaval: Fancy-dress balls; the 'Burial of the Sardine' parade in the Casa de Campo marks the changeover from *Carnaval* to Lent.
Easter Week *(Semana Santa)*: Solemn processions on Holy Thursday and Good Friday.
2 May: Celebrations on Plaza del Dos de Mayo to recall the popular uprising of 1808.
8–15 May: Week of fiestas, music and dance in honour of the city's patron saint, San Isidro. Pilgrimage to the saint's hermitage. Highlight of the bullfighting season.
24 June: Fireworks in Retiro Park for Midsummer Eve.
End of June to middle of September: Summer festival of culture *(Verano de la Villa)* includes a colourful array of open-air concerts, film, theatre and dance at several different venues.
Mid-July: *Virgen del Carmen* festival in the Chamberí quarter.
7–15 August: Lively *castizo* fiesta in Lavapiés and La Latina *(Fiestas de San Cayetano y San Lorenzo, Fiesta de la Paloma)*.
10 September: *Virgen del Puerto* fiesta in the Campo del Moro.
End of October: *Festival de Madrid* with international theatre and dance groups.
9 November: Fiesta to mark the feast day of the city's patroness, the *Virgen de la Almudena*.

Semana Santa procession

On parade in Plaza Mayor

Cruzcampo
Cruzcampo

Food and drink

Opposite: café life in central Madrid

Cocido, callos and churros

Madrid will give you an appetite. Migrants from all over the Iberian peninsula have enriched the region's cuisine, with South Americans and Orientals adding a further exotic touch. Spain's capital boasts an incredible 5,000 restaurants and 23,000 *bares, cervecerías, mesónes, tascas* and *tavernas.* With so many places to choose from, both *madrileños* and visitors like to keep on the move and change the scenery. No other subject receives more discussion than the question 'Where shall we eat and drink tonight'?

Breakfast *(desayuno)* never really poses any problems. It is usually just a quick *café con leche* (coffee with milk), plus perhaps a croissant, some toast and a glass of tap water to wash it all down. There is never any time in the morning for much more. Before the main midday meal, the substantial *almuerzo* (not served before 2pm), *madrileños* will graze on a few *tapas (see page 80)* accompanied perhaps by a draught beer *(caña)* or a glass of wine *(chato de vino)* while standing up in the bar on the street corner. The evening meal *(cena)* is very unlikely to start before 9.30pm – in fact restaurants are rarely full by 11pm.

The complete breakfast

After a tour of all their favourite haunts, night owls welcome in the sunrise with a portion of *churros con chocolate*, a stick of batter deep-fried in oil, dunked in a cup of thick chocolate.

Madrid cooking comes into the *zona de los asados*, the gastronomic 'roasting zone' which includes the whole of Castile. Typical Castilian dishes are crispy suckling pig *(cochinillo)*, milk lamb *(lechazo)* or kid *(cabrito)*, meat so tender and rich in flavour that it literally melts in the mouth. The joints are roasted in the oven *(horno de asar)*, or sometimes baked in a clay pot to keep the juices in. Main courses are usually served with a salad and bread.

Local favourites include appetising stews such as *estofado* (beef ragout with tomatoes, onions and potatoes), *callos a la madrileña* (tripe with black sausage, pepper sausage and calf's foot) and the almost obligatory *cocido madrileño.* After sampling such a typical winter evening meal as this Madrid speciality, few people want anything more – it is so filling. The dish consists of bacon, ham, chicken, black sausage, pepper sausage (*morcilla* or *chorizo),* potatoes, carrots and cabbage boiled in the pot along with soaked chick peas *(garbanzos)* and generally served with crisp chunks of bread for dunking and a robust red wine. The rich juices are drained off and served with some noodles as a soup. Once the meal for Madrid's poor, *cocido* now features on the menu in many top-class restaurants.

Lunchtime treats

Lighter, more digestible fare is supplied by the Atlantic Ocean. Freshly-landed fish from the north coast is delivered to Madrid overnight. Basque, Galician and Asturian restaurants have a reputation for fine fish cuisine. Among the most sought-after creations are *merluza a la gallega* (hake braised in a clay pot), *besugo al horno* (baked sea bream), *bacalao al pil-pil* (dried cod in a pepper sauce), *pulpo a feira* (boiled octopus) or *gambas al ajillo* (prawns in garlic oil). Many of the rice dishes associated with the Mediterranean region appear on menus in Madrid. *Paella*, the celebrated Valencian rice dish made with assorted shellfish and chicken, can be delivered to the door as *telepaella*.

Favourite desserts include *flan* (crème caramel), *leche frita* (thick bread and butter pudding), *mazapán* (marzipan from Toledo) and *tarta helada* (ice-cream tart).

Perhaps not to everyone's taste is *cabrales*, the strongly flavoured Asturian cheese (made from ewe's and goat's milk); a mature *queso manchego*, a ewe's cheese from the Mancha, has a very distinct taste. Cheese is often eaten together with *dulce de membrillo*, a quince paste cut into thin slices.

No meal is complete without a black coffee *(café solo)* or coffee with a little milk *(cortado)*; *carajillo* is coffee with a shot of brandy. The traditional way to conclude a fine meal is an *anisado*, an aniseed drink from Chinchón.

The local tipple

Wine selection

A typical bar

The red wines from the Madrid region *(Vinos de Madrid D.O.)* are little known elsewhere, but annual output is in the region of 40 million litres. The best quality wine is said to come from the Navalcarnero, Arganda and San Martín de Valdeiglesias vineyards. Bars and restaurants, however, are much more likely to offer lighter country wines from La Mancha (Valdepeñas, Almansa) and the highly-rated Riojas and Riberas del Duero. Vega Sicilia, from the banks of the Duero, is Spain's most expensive wine. The best white wines come from the Catalan Penedès region (Tarragona province).

Whatever the occasion, Andalusian *jerez* (sherry) goes down well, but *madrileños* tend to go for the drier varieties (*fino* and *manzanilla).*

Tapas

The origin of the long-standing Spanish tradition of the *tapa*, the tasty little snack to accompany a drink, is not entirely clear, but during the 13th century Alfonso the Wise, who was well known for his sobriety, ordered his thirsty soldiers to eat at least one piece of bread with every glass of wine. A similar instruction was given by Carlos III in the 18th century, to improve the constitu-

tion of the civil population. Other experts believe that it was the north African Berbers who brought the idea of a table full of various appetisers initially to Andalusia. The custom then spread across the whole Iberian peninsula.

Tapas bar

The *tapeo*, hunting for a tasty nibble, is as inseparable from the daily routine of the *madrileño* as Goya is from the Prado. In late afternoon and towards sunset, the ritual excursion to Huertas, Lavapiés or Chueca begins. The bars here keep the desirable delicacies behind glass windows: *boquerones en vinaigre* (pickled anchovies), *orejas a la plancha* (grilled pig's ears), *pimientos de padrón* (spicy peppers), *alitas* (chicken wings), *almejas* (cockles), *caracoles* (snails), *champiñones al ajillo* (mushrooms with garlic), *chicharrón* (roast ham) or *rabo de toro* (braised tail of bull) – the list of tempting little snacks is almost endless.

Tapas choices

A genuine *tapa* (lid) is actually a free offering by the barman to accompany a beer *(caña)* or a wine *(copita)*. It could be a piece of spicy sausage, cheese, fish, a bread roll or even just a bowl of olives or almonds – whatever happens to be available.

The *pincho*, a relative of the *tapa*, could be a small slice of *tortilla* (a potato and onion omelette), a grilled aubergine or a pickled pepper on a cocktail stick. However a *ración* (portion), often a larger meal, must be ordered in the usual way. *Una de gambas, otra de callos*... the words barely need to be spoken, before the plate slides silently over the bar.

Every *madrileño* has his or her own theory about where the best *tapas* are served – and it constantly needs to be put to the test. Maybe *tapeo* is related to the old hunting and gathering instinct. Whatever it is, do not allow yourself to be mistaken into thinking that *raciones* are cheaper than a meal served in a restaurant. Going on a *tapas*-crawl is an expensive way of passing the time.

Option at Puerto del Sol

Restaurant selection

These suggestions for restaurants in Madrid are listed according to the following categories: $$$ = expensive; $$ = moderate; $ = inexpensive.

Top of the range

Zalacaín, Álvarez de Baena 4, tel: 91-561 4840; Metro: Rubén Darío. One of the best (and most expensive) restaurants in Spain. Winner of many gastronomic awards. Specialises in Basque cuisine. Closed Saturday evening and Sunday. $$$.

Jockey, Amador de los Ríos 6, tel: 91-319 2435; Metro: Colón. Traditional, high-class restaurant. English-style interior, but Spanish cuisine with an international input. Closed Sunday. $$$.

O'Pazo, Reina Mercedes 20, tel: 91-553 2333; Metro: Nuevos Minis. Outstanding quality Cantabrian/Galician fish dishes. Closed Sunday. $$$.

Julián de Tolosa, Cava Baja 18, tel: 91-365 8210; Metro: La Latina. Basque/Navarre fare. Exquisite vegetable garnishes, e.g. *pimientos al piquillo*, served with meat. $$

The night is yet young

Traditional Madrid

La Bola, Bola 5, tel: 91-547 6930; Metro: Santo Domingo. Old Town restaurant famous for its *cocido* from the clay pot. Closed Sunday. $$.

Botín, Cuchilleros 15-17, tel: 91-366 4217; Metro: Sol. The oldest and best-known restaurant in town. Castilian specialities, e.g. *cochinillo asado* (roast suckling pig). $$.

Carmencita, Libertad 16, tel: 91-531 6612; Metro: Chueca. In García Lorca's local (founded 1850). Try the Basque-style *merluza* (hake). $$.

Casa Ciríaco, Mayor 84, tel: 91-548 0620; Metro: Sol. Still a classic venue, this is a preferred meeting place for

Chefs in action

politicians and artists. Good plain cooking – but *pepitoria de gallina* (chicken fricassée) is a speciality. Closed Wednesday. $$.

Casa Paco, Puerta Cerrada 11, tel: 91-366 3166; Metro: Sol. Tavern founded in 1870. Meat dishes in large portions. Closed Sunday. $$.

Casa Lucio, Cava Baja 35, tel: 91-365 3252; Metro: La Latina. Classic Castilian fare. No chance of a table if you don't book. Closed Saturday lunchtime. $$.

El Puchero, Larra 13, tel: 91-445 0577; Metro: Bilbao. Good *comida casera* (plain cooking), including various stews. Very popular. $$.

Casa Mingo, Paseo de la Florida 2, tel: 91-547 7918; Metro: Príncipe Pío. Draught Asturian cider *(sidra)*, roast chicken and *chorizo*. Noisy, popular and good fun. Often hard to find a vacant table. $.

Malacatín, Ruda 5, tel: 91-365 5241; Metro: La Latina. Rustic-style Old Town tavern with unbeatable portions of the best *cocido* in town (open lunchtime only). $.

Viuda de Vacas, Cava Alta 23, tel: 91-366 5847; Metro: La Latina. Basic, unconventional tavern with young clientèle. Closed Sunday evening and Thursday. $.

Traditional Spanish

La Giralda III, Maldonado 4, tel: 91-577 7762; Metro: Núñez de Balboa. *Pescaíto frito* (fried fish) and other Andalusian specialities, also sold as *tapas*. Popular and inexpensive. Closed Sunday. $$.

Extremadura, Libertad 13, tel: 91-531 8958; Metro: Banco de España. Do try the *caldereta de cordero* (lamb ragout) and the Extremadura ham. Nicely decorated with tiled pictures. Not expensive. Closed Sunday evening and Monday. $$.

Casa Parrondo, Trujillos 4 and 9, tel: 91-522 6234; Metro: Opera. Rather kitschy furnishings, but substantial *fabada* (thick bean soup), *sidra (*cider*)*, *pulpo* and other Asturian delicacies. *Tapas* bar and restaurant. $$.

Centro Riojano, Serrano 25, 1st floor, tel: 91-575 0337; Metro: Serrano. Salt cod and meat dishes from the Rioja region, plus some select wines. $$.

El Caldero, Huertas 15, tel: 91-429 5044; Metro: Sol. Down-to-earth Murcian cooking, e.g. *caldero* (fish and rice stew). Closed Monday evening and Sunday. $$.

La Paella Real, Arrieta 2, tel: 91-542 0942; Metro: Opera. By the Teatro Real. Paella in all its many varieties. Inexpensive. $$.

La Arrocería, Orense 70, tel: 91-570 9360; Metro: Cuzco. Mediterranean cuisine from Valencia and Catalonia. Excellent rice dishes. $$.

El Granero de Lavapiés, Argumosa 10, tel: 91-467 7611; Metro: Lavapiés. Good regional vegetarian dishes. $.

Tucking in

International

La Pampa Centro, Bola 8, tel: 91-542 4412; Metro: Santo Domingo. Looks like a ski cabin, but great Argentinian steaks. Very succulent *bife de chorizo*. $$.

El Cuchi, Cuchilleros 3, tel: 91-366 4424; Metro: Sol. Mexican and international dishes. Jokey furnishings. Fun-loving waiters. $$.

Centro Cubano, Claudio Coello 41, tel: 91-575 8279; Metro: Serrano. In a Cuban club; *ropa vieja con frijoles*, fried bananas, daiquiris, etc. Closed Sunday. $$.

Al-Mounia, Recoletos 5, tel: 91-435 0828; Metro: Banco de España. The best Moroccan fare north of Gibraltar. $$.

A Brasileira, Pelayo 49, tel: 91-308 3625; Metro: Alonso Martínez. *Feijoada*, fish and meat Brazilian-style. $.

Décor diversity

Tapas, wine and beer

Taberna de Antonio Sánchez, Mesón de Paredes 13; Metro: Tirso de Molina. Founded by the eponymous celebrity bullfighter. Where bullfighting fans get together.

La Dolores, Plaza de Jesús 4; Metro: Atocha. Bright and friendly. Excellent marinated anchovy fillets. Not cheap.

Casa Alberto, Huertas 18; Metro: Antón Martín. Nice atmosphere. Established in 1827.

La Casa del Abuelo, Victoria 12; Metro: Sol. *The* place for *gambas a la plancha* since 1906.

El Brillante, Glorieta del Emperador Carlos V 8; Metro: Atocha. Huge selection of inexpensive rolls *(bocadillos)*. Always busy.

Casa Antonio, Latoneros 10; Metro: Sol. Authentic *taberna* with local colour; *callos, champiñones*, etc.

La Oreja de Oro, Victoria 9; Metro: Sol. Simple, cheap, good. Specialities: *oreja* (pig's ear) and *navaja al la plancha* (jack-knife clam).

Casa Labra, Tetuán 12; Metro: Sol. Where the Spanish Socialist party (PSOE) was founded in 1879. Specialities: *bacalao (*dried cod) and *croquetas* (croquettes).

La Venencia, Echegaray 7; Metro: Sol. Sherry and olives in a *taberna*. A museum piece in itself.

Cervecería Alemana, Plaza Santa Ana 6; Metro: Sol. Founded by German settlers. Popular starting point for a night out.

Almendro 13, Almendro 13; Metro: La Latina. Young clientèle. Unusual selection of *tapas*.

Teatriz, Hermosilla 15; Metro: Serrano. Chic designer bar and restaurant in theatre converted by Philippe Starck.

The bullfight theme

Café at Puerto del Sol

Cafés

Café del Círculo de Bellas Artes, Alcalá 42; Metro: Banco de España. Not restricted to members of the club. Magnificently old-fashioned.

Service with a smile

Café Comercial, Glorieta de Bilbao 7; Metro: Bilbao. Popular venue for Malasaña revellers.
Café Gijón, Paseo de Recoletos 21; Metro: Banco de España. Traditional meeting place for literary types.
Café de Oriente, Plaza de Oriente 2; Metro: Opera. Stylish Belle-Epoque café at the Teatro Real.
Nuevo Café Barbieri, Avemaría 45; Metro: Lavapiés. Dignified coffee-house but with a young clientèle.
El Espejo, Paseo de Recoletos 31; Metro: Banco de España. With a magnificent glass pavilion.

Terrazas

The French have the pavement café, the Germans have the beer garden, the *madrileños* the *terraza*. From the end of June, these open-air cafés and bars on the city's squares and boulevards are frequented by the locals who cannot get away for the summer.

Most of Madrid's *terrazas* are situated by Paseo de la Castellana, Calle Serrano and Paseo del Pinto Rosales (Parque del Oeste) and are usually decked out in typical beach bar style. But customers are not relaxed by the sound of waves rippling on the shore. In the background is the roar of traffic... and in Madrid that continues until well into the early hours.

The southern section of Castellana is sometimes referred to as *La Costa Madrileña*. During the 1970s and 1980s, these cafés were very popular with bohemians, but now the clientèle is rather more prosperous. During the long summer nights, beauty contests, fashion shows and themed fiestas are held to entertain the crowds. At the end of the *movida* era (*see page 89*), many of the bars had to close. For the local residents the nocturnal habits of these outsiders became too much to bear and careless parking blocked the traffic. The *terrazas* have not been banned; there are just not so many of them nowadays.

Typical terraza

Alcalá shops

Shopping

In the scorching heat of summer, browsing in an air-conditioned shopping mall or a department store becomes a pleasure. The top names in fashion, from Armani to Yves Saint-Laurent, are found in the Salamanca quarter on Calle Serrano, Calle Ortega y Gasset and Calle Goya. Shoppers with less sophisticated tastes should explore the area between Gran Vía and Puerta del Sol, in particular the traffic-free Calle de Preciados and Calle del Carmen. There are numerous traditional Madrid stores around Plaza Mayor and in the Huertas and Lavapiés districts. The best time for bargains *(rebajas)* is usually between the end of June and the middle of July, just before the *madrileños* disappear for their summer break.

City centre illuminations

Antiques and handicrafts

Amieva-México, Huertas 17; Metro: Sol. Prints, etchings and books.

Galerías Piquer and **Nuevas Galerías**, Ribera de Curtidores 12/29; Metro: La Latina. Shops where you can have a good rummage around. In the heart of the Rastro quarter. Look out for Art Deco articles in Siglo 20.

Almirante 23, Almirante 23; Metro: Chueca. Old postcards, photographs and curios.

El Arco de los Cuchilleros, Plaza Mayor 9; Metro: Sol. Traditional pottery, porcelain and silverware.

El Caballo Cojo, Segovia 7; Metro: Sol. Spanish folk art, pottery, glass, etc.

Rastro hardware

Bric-à-brac and crafts of all kinds are on sale every Sunday at the **Rastro** flea market *(see page 45)*, but many art and antiques dealers are open throughout the week in the same area and also in Calle del Prado.

Galleries

Soledad Lorenzo, Orfila 5, tel: 91-308 2887; Metro: Colón. One of Madrid's leading galleries; devoted to Spanish and international avant-garde.
Antonio Machón, Conde de Xiquena 8, tel: 91-532 4 093; Metro: Chueca. Established modern Spanish artists.
Tiempos Modernos, Arrieta 17, tel: 91-542 8594; Metro: Opera. Contemporary photography, sculpture, graphics.

Music

El Flamenco Vive, La Unión 4; Metro: Opera. Flamenco records, CDs, books, musical instruments etc.
Félix Manzanero, Santa Ana 12; Metro: La Latina. Well-known guitar-maker.

Food and drink

Lhardy, Carrera de San Jerónimo 8; Metro: Sol. Top-class delicatessen and restaurant ($$$).
El Madroño, Caravaca 10; Metro: Lavapiés. Jams, liqueurs, sweets – anything that can be made from the fruit of the strawberry tree *(madroño)*... and other delicacies.
Mariano Madrueño, Postigo de San Martín 3; Metro: Santo Domingo. An outlet for fine wines, liqueurs, brandies and spirits since 1895.
Almacén de Licores David Cabello, Cervantes 6; Metro: Antón Martín. A typical *bodega*. Current wine and brandy offerings displayed on a blackboard.
La Oleoteca, Juan Ramón Jiménez 37; Metro: Plaza de Castilla. The finest olive oil in Spain.
La Violeta, Plaza de Canalejas 6; Metro: Sol. Tiny shop all in lilac to match the wide range of Parma violets.
Pastelería El Riojano, Calle Mayor 10; Metro: Sol. Famous cake shop.
Palacio de los Quesos, Calle Mayor 53; Metro: Sol. All kinds of Spanish cheese with wines to match.
Museo del Jamón, eg Gran Vía 70; Metro: Plaza de España. Bar, restaurant and delicatessen all in one. Many branches. Excellent hams.

The real Madrid

Casa de Diego, Puerta del Sol 12; Metro: Sol. Fans, walking sticks and parasols.
Casa Yustas, Plaza Mayor 30; Metro: Sol. Every kind of hat, including the *boina* (Basque-style beret).
Seseña, Cruz 23; Metro: Sol. *Capas* (round cloaks made from flannel and felt) made to measure – for him and her.
Plata Joyas López, Prado 3; Metro: Sol. Huge selection of traditional silverware.
Corsetería La Latina, Toledo 49; Metro: La Latina. Lingerie and corsets, exclusively for the larger woman.
Casa Jiménez, Preciados 42; Metro: Callao. Fans, *man-*

Browsing in the Lhardy

Something fishy

Museo del Jamón

tillas (lace veils) and *mantones de manila* (shawls).
Guantes Luque, Espoz y Mina 3; Metro: Sol. Gloves, made-to-measure if required.
Calle de Libreros; Metro: Callao. 'Street of booksellers'.

Fashion

Ekseption, Velázquez 28; Metro: Velázquez. Beautifully-presented fashions for *señoras* and *señores*.
Sybilla, Jorge Juan 12; Metro: Retiro. One of Spain's leading women's fashion designers. Smart and expensive.
¡Oh, qué Luna! Ayala 32; Metro: Velázquez. Lingerie, pyjamas, bed-linen.
Adolfo Domínguez, Ortega y Gasset 4; Metro: Núñez de Balboa. Modern men's fashions. Steep prices.
Zara, Carretas 6, Preciados 20 and elsewhere; Metro: Sol. Chain for young fashions at modest prices.
Calle del Almirante, Metro: Chueca. Contemporary clothes for him and her.

Shoes and leather

Antigua Casa Crespo, Divino Pastor 29; Metro: San Bernardo. *Alpargatas* (rope-soled canvas shoes) galore.
Camper, Gran Vía 54; Metro: Callao. Fashionable and casual shoes.
Lotusse, El Jardin de Serrano Goya 6; Metro: Serrano. Classic footwear for men and women.
Lurueña, Gran Vía 60 and elsewhere; Metro: Plaza de España. Branded shoes, often at greatly reduced prices.

M&S

Department stores

El Corte Inglés, Preciados 3 and elsewhere; Metro: Sol.
Galerías Preciados, Plaza del Callao; Metro: Callao.
Marks & Spencer, Serrano 52; Metro: Serrano.
FNAC, Preciados 28; Metro: Callao. CDs, books, software, newspapers and magazines.
VIPS, Gran Vía 42 and 14 branches; Metro: Callao. Newspapers, magazines, books, CDs, gifts, etc... open until 3am.

ABC Serrano

Shopping centres

ABC Serrano, Serrano 61; Metro: Núñez de Balboa. Popular bar and restaurant on the roof terrace.
El Jardín de Serrano, Goya 6–8; Metro: Serrano. Fashions and jewellery in an elegant setting.

Antón Martín market

Markets

La Cebada, Plaza de la Cebada; Metro: La Latina. The largest market in the Old Town.
San Miguel, Plaza de San Miguel; Metro: Sol. Attractive ironwork structure.
Antón Martín, Santa Isabel 5; Metro: Antón Martín. Pleasant local market.

La Fontana taverna

Nightlife

Viva la noche

Madrid me mata – Madrid is killing me, the deep and dramatic sigh associated with *la movida* – the early 1980s movement, nurtured by the socialist mayor, Enrique Tierno Galván, which saw popular traditions re-emerge and youth culture explode – still has a ring of truth. Where else in Europe is traffic at a standstill at 4 am? Constantly in search of the ultimate in entertainment, it is not just groups of young people who flock into the city centre after work, usually from Thursday to Saturday and at least until sunrise. The motto is *¿Adónde vamos?* – 'So where now?'

The main themes seem to be having fun, making contact and flirting, but also staying on the move. Good starting points for an evening stroll are the *cervecerías* on the Plaza Santa Ana, the *terrazas* *(see page 85)* along the Castellana or the *tascas* and *tavernas* in the arty Huertas quarter, where you can have a bite to eat before things really get going in the clubs, bars and discos.

As well as offering the opportunities for socialising, eating and drinking, Madrid nightlife provides a wealth of cultural experiences. To find out what is on, consult the magazine *Guía del Ocio,* out every Friday and available in kiosks. Another guide, *Qué hacer – What's on*, is available in hotels and at tourist offices. Advanced ticket sales: Caja de Cataluña, tel: 915 383 333. Payment by credit card.

One club among many

Teatro Español

Opera, theatre and ballet

Teatro Español, Príncipe 25, tel: 914 296 297; Metro: Sol. Classical and modern dramas.
Teatro Real, Plaza de Oriente 4, tel: 915 160 660; Metro: Opera. The opera house was finally opened in 1997.
Teatro de la Zarzuela, Jovellanos 4, tel: 915 245 400;

Metro: Banco de España. Opera and ballet from January to July, *zarzuelas* from October to December.
Teatro Albéniz, Paz 11, tel: 915 318 311; Metro: Sol. Comunidad de Madrid's respected theatre.
Sala Olimpia, Plaza de Lavapiés, tel: 915 274 622; Metro: Lavapiés. Modern plays under the direction of the National Dramatic Centre.
Teatro de la Comedia, Príncipe 14, tel: 915 214 931; Metro: Sevilla. Classical Spanish and international plays.

Teatro de la Comedia

Concert halls

Auditorio Nacional de Música, Príncipe de Vergara 146, tel: 913 370 140; Metro: Cruz de Rayo. Home of the national orchestra.
Teatro Monumental, Atocha 65, tel: 914 298 119; Metro: Antón Martín. Radio Televisión Española's symphony orchestra.

Flamenco (tablaos)

Café de Chinitas, Torija 7, tel: 915 595 135; Metro: Santo Domingo. Directed mainly at tourists. Performance quality varies. Meals served in the *tablaos*. Booking essential.
Casa Patas, Cañizares 10, tel: 913 690 496; Metro: Antón Martín. For connoisseurs. Climax well after midnight.
Corral de la Morería, Morería 17, tel: 913 658 446. The dancer, Rosario Castro *La Charola*, is a big star.
Torres Bermejas, Mesonero Romanos 11, tel: 915 323 322; Metro: Callao. Musically outstanding, though the pseudo-Moorish interior is not to everyone's taste.

Jazz and Latin

Café Central, Plaza del Ángel 10; Metro: Sol. Nice restaurant in coffee-house style. International programme.
Café Populart, Huertas 22; Metro: Antón Martín. Jazz and blues live.
Clamores, Albuquerque 14; Metro: Bilbao. Jazz, folk and Spanish singer-songwriters.
Café del Mercado, Ronda de Toledo 1; Metro: Puerta de Toledo. Salsa and merengue.

Maravillas – a popular disco

Clubs and discos

Archy, Marqués de Riscal 11; Metro: Rubén Darío. Top disco. The place to be seen.
Joy Eslava, Arenal 11; Metro:Sol. Disco in an old theatre.
Tranvía, Caballero de Gracia 20; Metro: Gran Vía. Flamenco upstairs, soul, funk and techno downstairs.
Palacio de Gaviria, Arenal 9; Metro: Sol. Disco for accomplished duos. Salsa very popular. Worth watching.
Kapital, Atocha 125; Metro: Atocha. Mega-disco on seven storeys. Films, karaoke and a whole host of extras for kids.
La Riviera, Paseo Bajo de la Virgen del Puerto; Metro:

Príncipe Pío. Live concerts, disco. Sunday is salsa day.
Soul Kitchen, Mesonero Romanos 13; Metro: Callao. Acid jazz, funk and hip-hop. Mixed clientèle.
Palace, Plaza Isabel II 7; Metro: Opera. Unusual dance hall with orchestra. Table telephones for making contact.
Sirocco, San Dimas 3; Metro: Noviciado. Rock, jazz and alternative Spanish.
El Sitio, Costanilla de los Angeles 20; Metro: Santo Domingo. Salsa, cumbia and merengue.
Galileo Galilei, Galileo100; Metro: Argüelles. Varied cultural events (live music, theatre and cabaret), plus bar.
Suristán, Cruz 7; Metro: Sol. Interesting café-theatre.
La Vía Láctea, Velarde 18; Metro: Bilbao. A *movida* era leftover, in fashionable Malasaña. Garage rock and pop.
Maravillas, San Vicente Ferrer 35; Metro: Tribunal. Club with contemporary pop music, sometimes live.

Bars and pubs

Los Gabrieles, Echegaray 17; Metro: Sol. Magnificent tiled surroundings. Good music. A must.
Viva Madrid, Manuel Fernández González 7; Metro: Sol. Very popular with *madrileños* and tourists. Not cheap.
Villa Rosa, Plaza de Santa Ana 15; Metro: Sol. *Azulejos*-adorned music bar (open until 4am).
Cock, Reina 16; Metro: Gran Vía. Legendary venue since the days of Buñuel. Once a brothel, now a trendy bar with marble fireplace, columns and high ceilings. Expensive.
Chicote, Gran Vía 12; Metro: Gran Vía. Hemingway's regular haunt. Good cocktails, antiquated furnishings.
Heaven, Veneras 2; Metro: Santo Domingo. Disco popular with gays, but not exclusively so.

Familiar signs

Other attractions

Casino Gran Madrid, Carretera La Coruña (29km/18 miles from Madrid). Roulette, blackjack and disco. Shuttlebus from Plaza de España 4pm–5am.
Hipódromo de la Zarzuela, Carretera La Coruña (8km/5 miles from Madrid). Evening horse-racing, 10.30pm–2am Saturday and Sunday, *terrazas* and live music. Shuttlebus from Moncloa metro station.
Noches del Cuplé, Palma 51; Metro: Noviciado. Olga Ramos sings traditional *cuplés, chotis* and *pasodobles.*
Scala, Hotel Melía Castilla, Capitán Haya 43; Metro: Cuzco. Extravagant dinner shows, Moulin Rouge-style.
Filmoteca Española *(Cine Doré)*, Santa Isabela 3; Metro: Antón Martín. Films for serious movie-buffs. Two halls.
Open air cinema for the *Verano de la Villa* on Paseo de la Florida, near Ermita San Antonio.
Chocolatería San Ginés, Pasadizo de San Ginés 5 (near *Joy Eslava*); Metro: Sol. The classic finale to a night out on the town. Great *churros*, hot chocolate (open until 7am).

VAGON CUBA
PROPIEDAD DE ESTA
CASA PARA LA IMPORTACION
de sus VINOS
FELIPE MARIN y H.NOS
VINOS y AGUARDIENTES
CALLE Sn. VICENTE Nº 44
Teléfono 24420
TARA 15730
NORTE
V. Moreno

Getting There

Opposite: tiles at Atocha station

By air

Madrid's Barajas airport, located just 16km (10 miles) out of the city, is one of Europe's six leading airports for passenger traffic. There are scheduled flights to England via British Airways and Iberia (now merged), and also services to the United States by Iberia, TWA, Continental, United, Delta and American Airlines.

The international departures terminal has a large cafeteria, post office and left-luggage facilities. For flight information, call 91-305 8343/4/5.

Barajas airport

A bus service runs every 12 to 20 minutes (depending on the time of day) to the underground bus terminal at the Plaza Colón in the heart of the city (400 Ptas; every 15 minutes from 4.45am to 1.30pm). The city centre can also be reached on the new underground line 8 (opened in 1999), but passengers still have to change at least twice.

Official Madrid taxis are white with red stripes across the doors. Expect to pay about 2,200 Ptas for the journey from the airport into the city. If you think you have been overcharged, ask for a receipt *(recibo oficial)* and note the driver's licence number *(see page 94)*.

Most big car-hire companies have offices at the airport.

By train and bus

Train to Toledo

Trains from the north arrive at Chamartín, Madrid's modern railway station (tourist information available; Metro link). Trains to southern Spain, e.g. the AVE express to Córdoba and Seville leave from Estación de Atocha. Most local traffic runs from Príncipe Pío station. For train information (RENFE), call 91-328 9020.

Most long-distance coaches arrive at Estación Sur (Metro: Méndez Alvaro). Their route network covers all of Spain. Fares are cheap and coaches comfortable and air-conditioned. For information, call 91-468 4200.

By car

The road journey from London and northern Europe takes at least 24 hours (in a fast car, without an overnight break). Allow six hours from the Spanish border at Irún to Madrid. Drivers will need a green card, their vehicle registration document and a bail bond; an international driving permit is recommended. Tolls are payable on Spain's motorways.

By sea

The convenience of a ferry from Plymouth to Santander or Bilbao must be balanced against the cost and, in winter, the risk of cancellation due to bad weather. Plymouth to Santander (Brittany Ferries) takes 24 hours; Plymouth to Bilbao (P&O Stena Line) involves two nights on board.

Plaza de la Cibeles

Getting Around

Taxi fares are cheap

By taxi

Madrid boasts about 15,500 taxis. If you need one, simply wave the driver down. Fares are relatively cheap; a ride in the city will rarely cost more than 1,000 Ptas. When you enter the car, the taximeter should be set at 180 Ptas, with surcharges payable for luggage, the airport, the trade fair centre and railway station destinations, on Sundays and also journeys late at night. Tariffs must be shown in the rear right-hand window.

Passengers unhappy with the service they receive can go to the taxi complaints office in the Town Hall (Plaza de la Villa, tel: 91-447 0714).

By public transport

The reliable Metro

By far the most reliable form of transport in the city is the Metro. The trains on the 11 lines run every day from 6am to 1.30am, while 151 bus routes operate from 6am to midnight. A night service (*búhos* = owls) operates until 5am from Puerta del Sol and Plaza de la Cibeles. There is a standard fare of 130 Ptas per single journey *(sencillo)*, but there is a clear saving if you buy one of the 10-trip tickets *(Metrobús)* for only 680 Ptas. The Metrobús ticket is valid for all urban buses and is available from all metro stations. Bus drivers only sell single tickets. For Metro information, call 91-552 5909, for buses 91-401 9900.

By car

Even those who have travelled to Madrid by car will probably be glad of the opportunity to let someone else take the wheel when it comes to exploring the city. In any event, they will save time – and their nerves – by using public transport. Congestion and shortage of parking spaces are all part of everyday life in Madrid. Illegally parked cars will be towed away. It may be possible to find space in one of the following central car parks: Cuesta de Santo Domingo, Plaza de las Cortes, Plaza de las Descalzas, Plaza de España, Plaza Mayor, Plaza de Santa Ana.

Sightseeing/Excursions

A double-decker bus operated by **Madrid Visión** plies five times a day between the main city sights. The tour begins at Calle San Bernardo 19 (corner of Gran Vía). A ticket costs 2,200 Ptas per person, but once you have bought it, you can interrupt your journey at any of the 14 stops as often as you like. Commentary is available in English through headphones.

Also worth investigating are the themed guided tours organised by the Patronato de Turismo *(see page 98)*. Popular themes include classical taverns and literary Madrid. The tours are currently conducted in Spanish only.

Sightseeing by bus

The following coach companies organise day-trips *(see page 66)*: **Juliátur**, Gran Vía 68, tel: 91-559 9605; **Pullmantur**, Plaza de Oriente 8, tel: 91-541 805; **Trapsatur,** San Bernardo 23, tcl: 91-541 6320.

Car-rental companies Most of the internationally known car-rental companies have offices at the airport, but hotel receptions will normally make all the necessary arrangements. Payment by credit card.

Fly-drive packages are available from the UK.

The Strawberry Train

The Spanish railway company RENFE has revived the historic Madrid to Aranjuez line, and every Saturday and Sunday (from April to October) a steam locomotive hauls what is known as the *Tren de las Fresas* or the Strawberry Train.

When it opened in 1851, the line was used for transporting fruit and vegetables to Madrid from the fertile pastures near the royal summer residence. Nowadays hostesses dressed in folk costume serve fresh Aranjuez strawberries to the passengers who sit in old-fashioned, panelled carriages

For further information, contact 90-222 8822. The fare, including the tasty refreshment and a ticket for a tour of the Royal Palace at the destination, is 3,250 Ptas.

The view from Faro de Moncloa

Cable-car panorama

Madrid from above

Madrid cannot boast any towering viewpoints such as the Eiffel Tower or Barcelona's Sagrada Familia, but if you look around, you will find a few places from where the vast extent of the city can be appreciated.

The roof terrace of the **Hotel Emperador** (Gran Vía 53; Metro: Callao), for example, offers a fine view of the Gran Vía. Furthermore, the inviting swimming pool is open to visitors (daily 11am–9pm; reduced admission from 3pm). The 92-m (300-ft) high **Faro de Moncloa** *(see page 32*; Metro: Moncloa) is used to observe traffic flow, but there is a glazed viewing platform which surveys the whole of western Madrid. The evening silhouettes of Plaza de España and the Royal Palace look like a huge film backdrop when viewed from the **Casa de Campo** cable-car cabins *(see page 32*; from Paseo del Pintor Rosales/Calle Marqués de Urquijo; Metro: Argüelles).

Superb sunsets and splendid panoramic views over the rooftops in the Old Town, as far as the skyscrapers of the AZCA quarter, are visible from the little-known **Parque del Cerro del Tío Pío** (Metro: Portazgo) in the east of the town. Another great view across to the Royal Palace and La Almudena cathedral can be enjoyed from the shady café terrace at **Las Vistillas** *(see page 29)* above Calle Segovia (on the corner of Calle de Bailén; Metro: Opera).

Route planning

Facts for the Visitor

Travel documents

Visitors from EU countries require only a valid national identity card to enter Spain. The same applies for citizens of Andorra, Austria, Liechtenstein, Monaco and Switzerland. As British citizens have no identity cards, they need a passport. Citizens of the United States, Australia and New Zealand also require a valid passport, and are automatically authorised for a three-month stay. Visitors from elsewhere must obtain a visa from the Spanish consulate in their own country before setting off. In Madrid,visitors may apply to extend a three-month stay for a further three months at the Comisaría de Policía, Sección de Extranjería, Calle Los Madrazo 9, tel:91-521 9350.

Customs

Visitors can bring the following items into the country duty-free: any personal effects, such as jewellery, cameras, film, video and sound equipment, musical instruments, sports equipment, etc, plus reasonable quantities of cigarettes (300 cigarettes for EU residents, 200 for the rest of Europe and 400 for non-Europeans), limited amounts of alcoholic beverages, perfumes, coffee and tea.

Tourist information

Spanish National Tourist Office (www.tourispain.es):
UK: 22-3 Manchester Square, London W1M 5AP, tel: 020-7486 8077; 24-hour brochure line: 09001 669 920;
US: 666 Fifth Avenue, 35th floor, New York 10021, tel: 212-265 8822; or 8383 Wilshire Bvd, Suite 960, 90211 Beverly Hills, California, tel: 213-658 7188/93; or 5085 Westheimer, Suite 4800, 77056 Houston, Texas, tel: 713-840 7412/3; or 845 N. Michegan Avenue, Suite 915, Chicago, Illinois 60611, tel: 312-944 0215/6.

Images of Madrid

Madrid
Oficina Municipal de Turismo, Plaza Mayor 3, tel: 91-588 1636.
Patronata Municipal de Turismo, Calle Mayor 69, E-28013 Madrid, tel: 91-588 2900, fax: 91-588 2930.
Comunidad de Madrid information offices: Aeropuerta de Barajas, tel: 91-305 8656; Duque de Medinaceli 2, tel: 91-369 7930; Metro: Sevilla; Estación de Chamartín, tel: 91-315 9976; Ronda de Toledo 1, tel: 91-364 1876.
Free municipal information line (Monday to Friday 8.30am–9.30pm): tel: 010; State tourist board *(Turespaña)* information line: tel: 90-130 0600.
Websites: www.munimadrid.com or www.madrid.org.

Toledo
Oficina de Turismo, Puerta de Bisagra, tel: 92-522 0843.

Avila
Oficina de Turismo, Plaza Catedral 4, tel: 92-021 1387.

Segovia
Oficina de Turismo, Plaza Mayor 10, tel: 92-146 0334.

Alcalá de Henares
Oficina de Turismo, Callejón Santa María 1, tel: 91-889 2694.

Telebanco ATM machines

Currency and exchange

The peseta (Pta) is the official Spanish currency. Notes are denominated in 1,000, 2,000, 5,000 and 10,000 pesetas, coins in 1, 5, 10, 25, 50, 100, 200 and 500 pesetas.The 5-peseta coins are known as *duros*.
Current exchange rate: £1 = 250 Ptas.

The easiest way to obtain cash is with a credit/ payment card and a PIN number at one of the many ATM machines *(telebanco)*. Most shops and restaurants accept credit cards, mainly MasterCard and Visa.

Almost all Spanish banks will change foreign currency and travellers' cheques, but charge a small commission.

Waiters expect tips

Tipping

Even for meals at all-in prices a 10 percent *propina* is normal. In a bar or café, leave a few coins for the waiter. When paying for a taxi, try to round up the fare.

Opening times

Shops and offices are generally open from 10am to 2pm and from 4 to 8pm. There are no statutory opening times. In the winter, siesta time is usually one hour shorter, but then the shops close earlier. Department stores and shopping centres do not normally close at lunchtime and are also often open on Sunday. Post offices open from 8am to 2pm. Museums close on Sunday afternoon and Monday, while many restaurants also shut on Sunday. Some cafés, restaurants and museums close during August.

Post-boxes are yellow

Public holidays

1 January, 6 January (Epiphany), 19 March (St Joseph's Day), Holy Thursday and Good Friday, 1 May, 2 May (Madrid Region Day), 15 May (San Isidro Day), 25 July (St James's Day), 15 August (Feast of the Assumption), 12 October (Columbus Day), 1 November (All Saints), 9 November (La Almudena Day), 8 December (Immaculate Conception), 25 December (Christmas).

Postal services

The General Post Office by Plaza de la Cibeles is open Monday to Saturday from 8am to 10pm. Stamps *(sellos)* are available at kiosks and tobacconists *(tabacos)*.

Telephone

It's good to talk

It is possible to make international calls from all public telephones. Phone cards *(tarjetas)* can be purchased at kiosks and tobacconists. At coin-operated phone booths, the smallest acceptable coin is 200 pesetas. The telephone office *(Telefónica)* at Gran Vía 30 is open daily from 9.30am to 11.30pm. Reduced tariffs for international calls are available from 10pm to 8am and all day Sunday.

To dial the UK from Spain, prefix your number with 00 44 and omit the first zero from the area code.

The dialling code for Spain is 00 34, and the area code for Madrid is 91.

Medical assistance

If an emergency arises, go to the accident and emergency department of a hospital *(Urgencias)* or summon help by dialling 112. For less urgent medical needs, ask at your hotel or tourist office for the name of a doctor, preferably English-speaking.

Although travellers from EU countries are advised to acquire the E111 certificate, which in theory entitles holders to take advantage of health facilities in any EU countries free of charge, it is much safer to have an accident and illness insurance policy. If you do need medical treatment, be sure to obtain a detailed invoice *(factura)* to present to your insurance company.

A green cross on a white background is the symbol for a pharmacist *(farmacias)*. Emergency opening times are published in daily newspapers.

Emergency dental service, *Clinica Dental de Urgencia:* Juan Bravo 44, 6th floor, tel: 91-402 6421 or 91-402 6422; 24-hour service, seven days a week.

Emergency numbers

061 Ambulance *(SAMUR)* or medical emergency *(Insalud)*
091 Police *(Policía Nacional)*
092 Municipal police *(Policía Municipal).*
080 Fire brigade *(Bomberos)*
91-522 2222 Red Cross *(Cruz Roja)*

There to protect

Lost property

Negociado de Objetos Perdidos, Plaza de Legazpi 7, tel: 91-588 4346; Metro: Legazpi.
Metro, bus or trains: Estación de Atocha, tel: 91-506 6969.

Crime

As in all major cities, it is essential to be on your guard against theft. Never leave valuables on view in a car and do not wear valuable jewellery or carry expensive camera equipment. Be especially vigilant in the Rastro flea market, in the metro, at night in the Malasaña quarter or on Gran Vía. Among the ruses often employed by pickpockets are street theatre artists who distract unsuspecting holidaymakers, staged accidents and fights.

Latest news

Newspapers

Many of the main Spanish daily newspapers, e.g. *El País*, *ABC*, *El Mundo* and *Diario 16*, are published in Madrid, and they contain listings pages with details of forthcoming cultural events. The weekly magazine *Guía del Ocio* also has a 'what's on' page. The TV station *Telemadrid* reports on events in and around Madrid. The state-owned *Radio 3* (FM 93.2) is popular with young people for its varied range of music – from free jazz to flamenco.

Trade fairs

Most trade fairs are held at the new Campo de las Naciones, which is situated close to Barajas airport. Information: IFEMA, Parque Ferial Juan Carlos I, Apdo. de Correos 67067, E-28067 Madrid; www.ifema.es.

Highlights from the trade fair calendar:
Mid-January and September: *Iberjoya* (clocks, watches and jewellery); end of January: *Fitur* (tourism); February: *Arco* (contemporary art); February and September: *Ibermoda* (fashion week); mid-March: *Expo Ocio* (leisure and sportswear); end of March and October: *Iberpiel* (leather goods and shoes); May: *Semana de la Alimentación* (food and drink); October: *Feria del Libro Antiguo* (books; on Paseo de Recoletos).

Diplomatic representation

UK: Fernando el Santo 16, tel:91-700 8200.
US: Calle Serrano 75, tel: 91-587 2510.

The Ritz

Accommodation

The range of hotels in Madrid is worthy of any capital city in the world. A fair number of inexpensive hotels are situated in the Barrio de los Literatos (Writers' Quarter) between Plaza Santa Ana and Plaza de las Cortes. Many hotels offer reduced weekend packages. In the more expensive hotels breakfast is usually included in the price: check when booking.

If you wish to book a hotel room from home, then a fax stating credit card number and expiry date is usually sufficient. Quality hotels can usually be booked through airlines and tour operators.

The Atlantico

Hostales and hotels

Accommodation in Madrid is graded, starting from the basic *Casas de Huespedes* (white CH on a blue plate), *Pensiones* (P), family-run *Hostales* (HS) to *Hotel*. Depending on facilities available, *hostales* are awarded up to three stars by the Turespaña tourist board.

Hotels are assessed and given a rating between one and five stars. At the moment only three hotels in Madrid are allowed to use the top designation of GL (*Gran Lujo,* or de luxe).

Hotel selection

These suggestions for hotels in Madrid are listed according to the following categories: $$$= expensive; $$= moderate; $= inexpensive.

Luxury hotels

Ritz, Plaza Lealtad 5, tel: 91-521 2857, fax: 91-532 3710; Metro: Banco de España. This has been Madrid's top hotel since 1910. Situated close to the Prado, it has 156 rooms, a lovely garden and a magnificent bar. $$$.

Santo Mauro, Zurbano 36, tel: 91-319 6900, fax: 91-308 5477; Metro: Rubén Darío. 37 luxury rooms and apartments in a renovated mansion. $$$.

Palace, Plaza de las Cortes 7, tel: 91-360 8000, fax: 91-360 8100; Metro: Sevilla. Belle Epoque establishment which still has the original stained-glass dome above the hotel lobby. $$$.

Wellington, Velázquez 8, tel: 91-575 4400, fax: 91-576 4164; Metro: Retiro. Regular haunt of celebrated bullfighters. $$$.

The Palace Hotel

The Fénix

Upmarket mid-range hotels

Ambássador, Cuesta de Santo Domingo 5, tel: 91-541 6700, fax: 91-559 1040; Metro: Santo Domingo. Centrally located; in an historic building, plush, but with affordable special rates. $$$.

Nacional, Paseo del Prado 48, tel: 91-429 6629, fax: 91-369 1564; Metro: Atocha. Brand new, effective design. Ideal for museum visits. $$$.

Miguel Angel, Miguel Angel 29–31, tel: 91-442 0022, fax: 91-442 5320; Metro: Rubén Darío. Very comfortable. Attentive service. $$$.

Fénix, Hermosilla 2, tel: 91-431 6700, fax: 91-576 0661; Metro: Colón. Lovely old hotel. Spacious rooms. $$$.

Crowne Plaza, Plaza de España, tel: 91-547 1200, fax: 91-548 2389; Metro: Plaza de España. Good location. Fully renovated city hotel. $$$.

Mid-range hotels

Emperador, Gran Vía 53, tel: 91-547 2800, fax: 91-547 2817; Metro: Callao. Right at the heart of things. Facili-

The Nacional

ties include swimming pool and terrace with view. $$$.
Arosa, Salud 21, tel: 91-532 1600, fax: 91-531 3127; Metro: Gran Vía. 1930s style. Renovated rooms. Quiet despite central position. $$.
Carlos V, Maestro Vitoria 5, tel: 91-531 4100, fax: 91-531 3761; Metro: Sol. Friendly and down-to-earth. Ask for one of the balcony rooms on the 5th floor. $$.
Opera, Cuesta de Santo Domingo 1, tel: 91-541 2800, fax: 91-541 6923; Metro: Opera. Outstanding position not far from the Royal Palace. $$.
Galiano, Alcalá Galiano 6, tel: 91-319 2000, fax: 91-319 9914; Metro: Colón. Small, delightful *hostal* with period furniture. Informal. $$.
Inglés, Echegaray 8, tel: 91-429 6551, fax: 91-420 2423; Metro: Sevilla. Pleasant atmosphere, in the heart of the writers' quarter. $.
Londres, Galdó 2, tel: 91-531 4105, fax: 91-531 4101; Metro: Puerta del Sol. In the pedestrianised zone. Modest and affordable. $.

Basic hotels
Cliper, Chinchilla 6, tel: 91-531 1700, fax: 91-531 1707; Metro: Callao. Off the Gran Vía. Friendly staff; good value. $.
Santander, Echegaray 1, tel: 91-429 6644, fax: 91-369 1078. Atmospheric old hotel. Simple rooms with high ceilings and large baths. Good location. $.
Europa, Carmen 4, tel: 91-521 2900, fax: 91-521 4696; Metro: Sol. Behind the Puerta del Sol. Well-run with friendly service. $.
Roma, Travesía de Trujillos 1 (Plaza de las Descalzas), tel: 91-531 1906. *Hostal* in a quiet but central position. Basic rooms with bath. $.
Hostal Cervantes, Cervantes 34, tel: 91-429 8365, fax: 91-429 2747; Metro: Antón Martín. Small and informal. $.

Aparthotel
Aparthotel Tribunal, San Vicente Ferrer 1, tel: 91-522 1455, fax: 91-523 4240; Metro: Tribunal. Studios with kitchenette. From 56,000 Ptas per week.

Youth hostels

Ricardo Schirmann, Casa de Campo, tel: 91-463 5699; Metro: Lago.
Santa Cruz de Marcenado, Santa Cruz de Marcenado 28, tel: 91-247 4732; Metro: Argüelles. In the student area.

Campsite

El Escorial, Carretera de Guadarrama, El Escorial, M-600, 3.5km (2 miles), tel: 91-890 2412, fax: 91-896 1062. Well-equipped campsite, 50km (31 miles) from Madrid.

Apartments at Puerto del Sol

Index